THE COMPLETE MANAGER'S GUIDE TO PROMOTIONAL MERCHANDISE

PROMOTING YOUR ORGANIZATION WITH PREMIUMS, FREEBIES, AND OTHER STRANGE BUT POWERFUL OBJECTS

THE COMPLETE MANAGER'S GUIDE TO PROMOTIONAL MERCHANDISE

PROMOTING YOUR ORGANIZATION WITH PREMIUMS, FREEBIES, AND OTHER STRANGE BUT POWERFUL OBJECTS

LOUIS THARP

Dow Jones-Irwin
Homewood, Illinois 60430

This publication is designed to provide accurate and authoritative information in regard to the subject matter covered. It is sold with the understanding that neither the author nor the publisher is engaged in rendering legal, accounting, or other professional service. If legal advice or other expert assistance is required, the services of a competent professional person should be sought.

From a Declaration of Principles jointly adopted by a Committee of the American Bar Association and a Committee of Publishers.

Sponsoring editor: Susan Glinert Stevens, Ph.D.
Project editor: Karen J. Murphy
Production manager: Bette K. Ittersagen
Jacket design: Tim Kaage
Compositor: Carlisle Communications, Ltd.
Typeface: 11/13 Century Schoolbook
Printer: Arcata Graphics/Kingsport

Library of Congress Cataloging-in-Publication Data

Tharp, Louis, 1951–
The complete manager's guide to promotional merchandise: promoting your organization with premiums, freebies, and other strange but powerful objects / by Louis Tharp.
p. cm.
Includes index.
ISBN 1-55623-212-8
1. Sales promotion. 2. Merchandising. I. Title.
HF5438.5.T52 1989
658.8′2—dc19 89–1580
CIP

Printed in the United States of America
1 2 3 4 5 6 7 8 9 0 K 6 5 4 3 2 1 0 9

To my family

FOREWORD

This book was originally to be titled *Chotzkies*. I made up the word with my research associate Ray Lamboy egging me on. Kathy Hegleman and Jim Bumgardner (two people who like me even more now that their names are in the book) found the spelling and definition of the original Yiddish word *Tshatshke*—a toy or trinket.

My editor, Dr. Susan Glinert, yawned. At our first meeting, she described a Chotzkie as "something you dust," not something you name a book aimed at corporate managers. But she has a way of letting a major argument like title verbiage work itself out.

It was worked out in an afternoon in Homewood, Illinois. The editorial board at Dow Jones-Irwin—which controls things like titles, book covers, and who knows what else—hated the made-up word *Chotzkie*. Susan called me with the news that the title was changed.

Focus groups, which I assembled and purposely peopled with what I thought would be psyches who would embrace the word, produced comments such as "Irritating"; "Don't know what it is"; "Is it Russian?"

Chotzkies the title died a quiet death, all references of it struck from the manuscript with a few keystrokes in the "Search and Replace" menu of the word processor.

Then Steven Goldmacher at North American Philips Lighting—two weeks before the manuscript was due—heard this made-up derivation of the word *Tshatshkes* for the first time and loved it. Steve's endorsement was not enough. By this time, even I was justifying the new title: "When you turn in your expense account with this book listed, nobody will question *The Complete Manager's Guide to Promotional Merchandise*. The same cannot be said for *Chotzkies*."

It's a good book anyway.

Louis Tharp

ACKNOWLEDGMENTS

This book is not an objective study of promotional merchandise. It is based on seven years' experience in the ad specialty industry. Although my formal training is in journalism, I am a part of the industry I write about. But I am not its cheerleader. I alone chose the case histories used in the book as well as the people quoted. I gravitated toward those people and companies that were forthcoming and easygoing about discussing their successes as well as their failures. Although I didn't like all the products or the promotional merchandise of all the companies I wrote about, I tried to be fair, including them because they help tell the story of an industry.

My target audience is buyers of promotional merchandise. So when I wrote about a product I felt was worthless, I said so. If I thought a certain company's promotions were worthless, I was a little more reserved in the company's favor. I assumed that I did not know what internal or external conditions may have helped contribute to a worthless campaign. As a reader, you will have no trouble distinguishing between the good and bad promotional merchandise programs, or why I think they deserve their respective labels.

The journalist in me, however, still gravitates toward fairness and objectivity, so it is unfortunate that the A.T. Cross Company, manufacturers of Cross writing instruments, refused to be interviewed for the book. Cross is mentioned—in a brief and unflattering light—in the chapter entitled *Gizmo Chaos*. The media relations consultant in me says Cross should have said its piece when it had the chance.

The corporations whose managers and executives did spend time providing information for this book and understanding what I really wanted, deserve my thanks and they have it. The companies as well as the people are too numerous to mention here, but are listed in the index.

Special thanks goes to Til Roemer at BMW of North America; Michael Redwine at Hard Rock Cafe; Steve Goldmacher at North American Philips Lighting; a lot of people at Golin/Harris Communications, Inc. in New York and Chicago including Ward White; Dr. James S. Gould, assistant chairperson, marketing, Lubin Graduate School of Business, Pace University; David Floyd of DJ Floyd & Partners Advertising, Indianapolis; Sara Basloe at Erickson/Basloe Advertising, New York; Greg Carrino, president of Alfa International; Deborah Hauss, Editor/Associate Publisher at Premium Incentive Business; and T-shirt maven John Caruso of St. Louis Sportswear in St. Louis.

Fred Danzig, editor at *Advertising Age* in New York, deserves special thanks for his willingness to allow a very successful column—The Next Trend—to be examined and nitpicked in Chapter 6 for its choice of promotional items awarded to readers as prizes. The different and unplanned twist this chapter took as I was writing it required an unusual dose of self-assuredness and an open-mind from Mr. Danzig. There are few magazines in the world, and even fewer editors, who would allow an author the latitude I got in preparing this chapter.

* * * *

The idea for this book came from Ray Lamboy, at the time an account executive at my firm, Clay Clay Steven & Blair. Ray—a few months out of college with a degree in communications—had heard me too many times on the phone apoplectic with suppliers who had shipped the geegaws late or printed the wrong color on the hat. He asked, after about a month on the job, how often promotional merchandise orders get screwed up. "Always," I answered. He retreated back to his media relations clients, where even in that virtually uncontrollable world, the odds were better.

When he was informed that he would have to become involved in the merchandising side of the business, he went to the library to research the subject. Two more visits to the library produced only 8 pages on promotional merchandise in a 400-page advertising textbook.

"You should write a book on this stuff," he said that Thursday afternoon. So we sat in front of the computer through the rest of the day and into the evening and wrote the chapter outline. The next day Ray had a list of 45 possible publishers—one of them Dow Jones-Irwin. We continued to work, constructing a market analysis. We found the market niche, and I wrote the first chapter, "Matching the Merchandise and the Message to the Market." Ray pronounced the chapter and the chapter outline acceptable. (He reads "how-to" and business books by the dozens—I don't.)

* * * *

Other people who deserve recognition include my editor Dr. Susan Glinert, my father—who began the business in 1981 when he wandered into the New York Premium show and decided it would be a good idea to try to sell imprinted Swiss Army knives, Jim Bumgardner, Dr. Rhoda Frindell Green, Bob Bruce, Lew Syken, Ann Tharp, Mark Kindley, Bill Wynn, Ellen Ruby, Pete Ligeti, Bea and Murray Fields, Andy Polansky, Dick Johnson, Claus Windelev, and Ed Waryas. Enthusiasm is their common trait. Their individual contributions are their distinctions.

L.T.

AUTHOR'S NOTE

Many of the companies mentioned in this book are my clients, but assuming you did not buy this book to get a veiled sales pitch from me, or to be impressed—or not—by a client list, I have not identified which are my successes and failures, and which are not.

L.T.

CONTENTS

CHAPTER 1

MATCHING THE MERCHANDISE AND THE MESSAGE TO THE MARKET

Situation: Many hospitals in the United States have found themselves in an unfamiliar competitive environment during the last five years. Community Hospitals—Indianapolis was no different. Its two med-check centers which handle non-life-threatening emergencies and a second hospital on the north side of Indianapolis were selected by management to participate in an inexpensive targeted-communications program.

The hospital's marketing department and its local advertising agency, DJ Floyd & Partners, identified newcomers to the Indianapolis area as a prime audience for the hospital sales message. Real estate agents were chosen as the messengers of the hospital message.

The message had to fulfill several image as well as sales objectives, and it had to have staying power. A newcomer might not need the services of Community Hospitals for several months or years, but when the need arose, Community wanted its name in front of the consumer.

Agency president David Floyd, a promotional merchandise disciple, decided a traditional brochure was the most effective and inexpensive way to tell the Community Hospitals story. But he also knew the useful life of the brochure was quite short once it got into the newcomer's hands. To improve the staying power of the hospital message, he matched the merchandise and the message to the market.

Doing this was as simple as gluing a thin magnet into the third page of the brochure. The magnet had a scale map showing med-check locations and a physician referral phone number. David knew that even though the newcomers might throw away the brochure, the magnet had a good chance of making it to the refrigerator door, where it would stay until it was needed. He knew that people rarely take magnets off their refrigerator.

THE MAGNET STUCK

To test the magnet's pulling power, 10,000 were given to newcomers through real estate agents. Demand for them was high, and follow-up surveys showed that the magnets made it to the refrigerator, where their message remained.

David was smart enough to look at the promotional merchandise as another media buy. The magnet had to fulfill the communications objective better than any other medium. It seems simple in retrospect, but it's the simple, inexpensive merchandise that can most often match the message and the market the way nothing else can. When someone does it right, as David did, the power of the gimmick is easily recognized.

Domino's Pizza uses refrigerator magnets successfully, too. The people at Domino's realized a long time ago that ordering a pizza often happens after you see nothing appealing in the refrigerator. A local Domino's phone number on the refrigerator, not necessarily by the phone, would have a great impact. The magnet is simply designed. The latest version has the name *Domino's,* the phone number for free delivery, and a line drawing of the Noid. It works time after time.

The reason promotional merchandise is so persuasive when used correctly is that it injects itself as a third component in the communications process. It is familiar and it performs a useful function, in addition to conveying a message. In the case of the magnets, nobody had to be told where to put them. They go on the refrigerator door where they hold notes, coupons, and school papers with gold stars.

As the third component, promotional merchandise complements the first two components—the message and the market—

which, in a good ad, are matched. When you use merchandise, match it to the message and the message to the market.

WALKING BILLBOARDS

In many cases where the merchandise is worn or displayed, the power of this type of communication is further enhanced. Now, instead of would-be consumers reading an ad in a magazine, they are reading the message on someone's hat or T-shirt, or on the bumper of a car. The term *participatory advertising* describes what is going on here. The user of your promotional merchandise wears your sales message and in doing so becomes part of the message as well as a potential customer. It doesn't take a Wharton M.B.A. to figure the exponential return in terms of positive exposures when each of 5,000 participatory advertisers wearing your logo and primary message on their shirt endorse this message in front of 5,000 more people. This is why participatory advertising impressions can be measured in parts of a penny instead of dollars per doodad.

In the print industry, these additional exposures are called *pass-along* or *secondary readership*—like when you look at someone else's *Sports Illustrated* swimsuit issue. Magazines in doctors' offices traditionally have a high pass-along rate because the people waiting there usually have nothing better to do than read four-month old periodicals.

When it comes to promotional merchandise, however, the equivalent of pass-along readership is a given. When the right hat is on the right head with the right message, you make a powerful and personal statement with exponential awareness returns (5,000 people each show 5,000 people your message). This kind of coverage makes the swimsuit issue circulation numbers look like a hockey score.

Conversely, when the wrong hat is on the wrong head, it's like pushing the "Door Close" button on an elevator—nothing happens.

The phenomenon of participatory advertising is overlooked by some otherwise very bright managers, independent businesspeople, and advertising agency executives.

OVERLOOKED, UNDERESTIMATED

One reason for this fact is negative inertia. Many communications professionals do not recognize the power of promotional merchandise, so there is a tendency to forget it during the planning stages of a communications program. Academics, too, don't seem to take this $24 billion a year industry seriously. One of the most popular advertising textbooks devotes only 4 out of 802 pages to promotional merchandise. The industry's salespeople tend to perpetuate this negative image, too. Most don't speak the latest advertising/marketing jargon, and very few even bother calling on agencies. Price, too, keeps this kind of merchandise out of many ad agency programs. Whatever it is, somebody else can get it cheaper. This makes promotional merchandise very ignorable to profit-conscious agencies.

If you participate in what could be called "giveaway snobbery," you can miss a powerful opportunity to communicate directly and personally with your constituencies, and in return receive their personal endorsement of your product or idea.

Smart advertisers know that grass-roots testimonials are the most powerful endorsement of a product; when you as a consumer use promotional merchandise, you are providing the company with a free testimonial.

Beverage, food, automotive, and insurance industries know the power of the pen with the message on its barrel, or the neon sign in the window of your favorite tavern. But, even here, promotional merchandise is not always integrated with advertising, public relations, or image campaigns so it can contribute to overall communications goals. Instead, it is often an adjunct to the sales effort, used as an inducement to increase the size of an order. This method may work, but it neglects the larger power of the merchandise, and it's expensive because the recipient attaches little value to the promotional merchandise in this environment. He looks at the merchandise as a freebie, a spiff, or a bribe. If you offer the spiff with the merchandise often enough, consumers will learn to expect it. They will not be motivated to buy without it. Marketers who use promotional merchandise as spiffs on a regular basis admit that customers learn to expect them. But these marketers justify their actions, saying they are simply compressing the time between giving out the merchandise and getting the sale. In the case of the Community Hospitals, the magnet might be around for a long time before the sale is made. When the beer distributor offers a flashing clock sign for a larger sale, the time interval between promotional merchandise and sale is the time it takes for the tavern owner to say, yes.

GETTING IT FOR FREE VERSUS BUYING IT FOR FREE

Time, or the absence of it, however, has an interesting way of changing our perception of promotional merchandise. If the cause and effect is known—getting the merchandise, buying the goods—as it is with disposable lighters packed with several packs of cigarettes, we tend to attach a harsher, more commercial meaning to the merchandise. By comparison, we tend to think of the Budweiser key tag we get free and use constantly as a gift with a message. We didn't have to buy a beer to get the key tag, but we are now more likely to buy a Bud voluntarily when the opportunity presents itself—without expecting another key tag. We may not, however, buy that particular brand of cigarettes again until we are offered another gimmick.

The message we give others is important, too. We are likely to describe the lighter as something we got for buying five packs of cigarettes. We use it as proof that we are a smart consumer, that we got something for nothing. The key tag, however, is likely to be described in the context in which it was given to us, using less commercial and more personal terms: "I got it at the mud bog race," or "They were giving them out at the state fair." We display it as proof that we belong to a special group. The commercial aspect, which everyone admits exists in both cases, is softened and redefined when there is a time interval between receiving the promotional merchandise and buying the related product. (Credit card companies have capitalized on this concept for years. Casinos replace your money with chips to keep you psychologically removed from the commercial aspects of your actions.) Keeping this distance between merchandise and sale also allows you, as a promotional merchandise buyer, to distinguish between the classic marketing use of the gimmick or giveaway, and the sales use of it as a point of purchase inducement. They may be the same promotional merchandise, but the message they can convey is very different.

The important point here is that as a purchaser of promotional merchandise, you are in a position to use it to your advantage to help you reach your communication, sales, advertising, image, or public relations goals. If you decide to use the merchandise as spiff, and are aware of spiff's positives and negatives, then you will make that decision with a good idea of resulting consumer reactions.

Like other forms of subtle persuasion and manipulation, there are few rules to follow when using promotional merchandise. It's like playing blackjack. If you win, you are considered a good player. If you lose, you are a poor player. Simply knowing that you can't go over 21 doesn't mean you'll be successful at the game. In some cases—as with promotional merchandise and blackjack—external factors beyond your control make you look better or worse than you actually are.

One example of these external forces is clearly illustrated in the spectacular and simultaneous promotional merchandise success and failure of the CAT™ hat. A simple baseball cap distributed by Caterpillar became de rigueur headgear for every midwestern teenager. The campaign extended into markets that had no intention of buying a Caterpillar product, but name recognition went through the roof. No one knows whether this contributed to increased sales. Caterpillar tractors are not a common purchase item. The hat took on a life and meaning of its own that had virtually nothing to do with the company's product line and everything to do with fashion.

NAPA, National Auto Parts Association, on the other hand, lives by the hat and controls whose head it covers. They are unofficially recognized in the promotional merchandise industry as the largest purchasers of baseball caps, and they keep them on the heads of buyers. The ubiquitous yellow caps with the royal blue and gold logo embroidered on a patch on the front of the cap has made its way into every service station, auto parts dealer, distributor and warehouser, gas station, car dealership, and auto race garage area in the western world. The name recognition—an important advertising objective for a company that relies on the same group of people purchasing products hundreds of times a year—is extremely high, but only among buyers. If you are not part of the automotive aftermarket industry, chances are you never knew what NAPA stood for, and may have never seen their hats before. It doesn't matter. NAPA knows how to reach its market. They do it through what one cap manufacturer calls "word of head advertising," and this strategy has worked for more than 20 years.

Like blackjack, the apparent simplicity of promotional merchandise hides complexity. When you pick a message messenger—someone to wear your hat or belt buckle—you have to make allowances for the unknown. If you can even partially control this media, however, and tap into the power of the promotional merchandise, you can reach old communications objectives in a new way. If you can't control it, you will wind up giving away a lot of golf balls that sit in golf bags and a lot of CAT™ hats that make a fashion statement without contributing anything positive to your profit and loss statement.

THEY SEEM SO SIMPLE, BUT . . .

Starting with the simplest merchandise, in an environment familiar to most people reading this book, I can take a few pages and make it complex. Watch. The promotional merchandise is a button. The environment is a trade show. Sounds simple? It's not.

First, when should you use buttons at a trade show? Only at a selling show, where your sales depend on semi-impulse buying. I use the word *semi-impulse* because the buyers would not be at the show if they were not prepared to buy. If the show is for lookers, forget the buttons.

A good example of a semi-impulse buyer's show is the National Stationery Show held in New York City. Here, stationers, gift shop, and boutique owners walk the aisles at the Jacob Javits Convention Center on Manhattan's west side, buying everything from Silly String™ in an aerosol can to greeting cards. Much of the buying is semi-impulse. If they see something they think will sell, they order it.

But, they have to see it first. And at the Javits Center, like all large exposition halls, buyers can miss a lot including your product and your booth.

You can use buttons to alert these buyers at the show that you have something to sell them. You can tell them what that something is and where they can get it immediately—period. The button is useless the minute the convention doors close each day.

THE FIRST STEP

The first decision to make is what will go on the button. Your name, your booth number, and your product. Imagine you are the product manager for a greeting card company and are pushing a special line at the show. A small replica of the card, which actually opens and is glued to the button, can have great impact. If you are introducing a new scent, then a scented button can tell your message. These two examples, and others that follow, assume the show is not three days away and you just remembered you needed giveaways for the show. A last-minute rush job with block letters in one color proclaiming the virtues of your product will not achieve the desired results. Few readers of a button like this will react positively, and you won't be able to get the most effective message messengers to wear it, either. Ironically, many of the same managers who spend weeks ruminating over an ad in a trade magazine that 15,000 passive readers will see once, will spend only 15 minutes writing copy for a button that 30,000 active buyers will see over and over during a trade show.

STEP TWO

A button's size is very important. In choosing the right size, ignore for a minute what you think would be a good size, and ignore the button price list. Ask these questions instead: Do the people who are going to read the button have good eyesight? Many people who wear reading glasses will not wear them when walking through the aisles of a trade show. When they go into a booth, they may or may not put on their glasses. I used to go to trade shows with a buyer who would not wear her glasses unless she was interested in reading the product information in the booth. The bigger and simpler the message on the button, the better. Figure that the viewers will have about two seconds to read your message, but that they will be exposed to it several times during the day. So they don't necessarily have to completely understand the message the first time around, but they can't be frustrated by it either. What is the largest button you can get away with? If the trade show is for the music industry and you are pushing Grateful Dead albums, the button can be big enough to roll down the aisles with a stick. If your market consists of surgeons, lawyers, accountants, or a similar group, the smaller and more tastefully subtle the button, the more likely they are to wear it. Rowdier groups can identify with flashing lights and off-color graphics.

Whatever the size, the message must wear well throughout the day, so it can't be too cute. Again, many people spend weeks compiling just the right verbiage for an ad, but ignore this discipline when writing copy for a button.

STEP THREE

Who wears your button is crucial to your image during the show. You want to select the participatory advertisers who will most effectively draw buyers into your booth so you can sell your product. These people wearing your button will become your message messengers. To make sure the right people are wearing your sales message, hire demographically correct people to give out the buttons at the door to the convention center at prescribed times.

For example, if you are selling the hypothetical new greeting card line, to who is it marketed? Grandparents? Yuppies? Carpenters? Use the same type of people to give out the buttons. Begin the continuity of your sales message now, when buyers first walk through the door. Which buyers do you want? Many shows have coded badges so exhibitors can zero in on hot buyers. Make sure your button people know what these codes mean so they can get to the hot buyers.

Besides having your demographically correct button distributors at the doors when the show opens, station them there again at mid-morning and then just after lunch. If the show runs into the evening, distribute the buttons after dinner. This staggered distribution pattern will insure that a constant number of people—the right message messengers—will be at the show walking the aisles and wearing your button at all times. Each day, give out enough buttons so that one-third of the people walking the aisles are wearing them. The one-third philosophy here is threefold. First, buyers won't become immune to your message as they might if everyone were wearing a button. Second, if you are selective about whom you want to represent your company, you probably couldn't give them out to more than a third of the people. Third, your participatory advertisers—the button wearers—must feel that they belong to a special group and that there is a special reason they are wearing the button.

Buttons, like sales opportunities, are perishable. Your goal is to create a one-day mystique in a closed system—the convention center—that results in customers seeking out your booth to buy your product.

SELECT YOUR MESSENGER CAREFULLY

This brings us to the point when the prospective customer walks into the booth, having seen the button, and instead of buying your product, asks for a button. At this point, if your sales force sees this person as a qualified buyer, they will know what to do with a warm body in a selling environment. But what about the button? If the person fits the demographics, give him or her a button. If not, give an inexpensive pen or a key tag. These people will be just as happy, but they will put it in their pockets and won't disrupt your image at the show. They will, however, have a positive feeling toward your product and your company, recommend your products, and show others—after the show—what they got from your booth.

If you're looking for a little extra punch from your button, ask your button distributors to check with the show organizers and find out if any famous people are stopping by the show. If so, the distributors should find the celebrity and pin a button on him or her. Make sure, too, that your selling people in the booth are wearing a button. If it helps achieve your objective, offer your buttons to the convention center employees. Under the right circumstances, seeing a button on the apron of an employee at the chili counter of Chicago's McCormick Place can help lunch-hour patrons remember to visit the booth right after they eat.

When you use promotional merchandise to achieve a marketing, sales, or communications goal like the one shown here, its value can be quantified. You won't feel like you're giving something away for free; rather, you'll know you are purchasing advertising space. And often in making this purchase, the lower priced items are most effective, as we have seen with the refrigerator magnets and buttons. It's how they are used, not how much they cost, that determines their value.

And, this brings us to the last point of this hypothetical greeting card company at the National Stationery Show. Don't put the buttons in a bowl in the booth. The purpose of the buttons is to persuade buyers on the floor to visit your booth. If they amble by, see your product and your buttons side by side, and come in for a button—you should give up greeting cards and consider going into the button business.

Suppose you like the persuasion of the button, but you believe your customers would respond more positively if you spent more money. Suppose there were a homing device in each button, and the receiver was at your booth. As people got closer to your booth, the buttons would start beeping faster and faster. If your show sales message was a take-off on the childhood game of "your getting hotter, hotter" and you transfer this "hotter, hotter" theme to your product, the buttons could create a lot of excitement at your booth. Another theme could center on the "home" part of the homing device: "Come home to our product."

The local media covering the show might be interested in something like this, too.

Another idea might be to put a clock in your button and use it to encourage buyers to visit your booth before a certain time. You might want to do this if you are at one end of the show floor and your biggest competitor is at the other end. You determine that it would take buyers starting at your competitor's end four hours to reach your booth. You are afraid they might have already bought from your competitor, or that they will forget about you. Use the buttons with a clock and offer a sales inducement to visit the booth within one hour of the show opening. If you don't mind complicating this a bit more and increasing the cost, stamp the buyers' hands or their badges with the time they arrive. If they visit your booth within a certain time after arriving, they receive the sales inducement. The message messengers wearing the clock buttons serve as a reminder to get to your booth before time runs out.

The button has other lives, longer than as a trade show staple. When the button identifies the wearer as a member of an ideological group, its life span is likely to be considerable. Political and cause promotional merchandise is a good example of this—the inexpensive bumper sticker and button often find their way into attics, antique shows, and high-priced auctions.

Nevertheless, the key to promotional merchandise, regardless of cost, is that all components—sales, marketing, image—must work together to form a cohesive message that causes action.

When you decide to use promotional merchandise thoughtfully to produce these results, you complicate your business life. First, there aren't many experts who can tell you what to do. Second, unlike an advertisement in a magazine, or a brochure, or a point of purchase display, you are relying on people to carry your message to buyers. This can seem like a risky way to get your message across, but the spectacular returns can make the perceived risk rewarding—as long as the merchandise matches the message and the message matches the market.

CHAPTER 2

WHAT MAKES A PROMOTIONAL MERCHANDISE ITEM GOOD?

The short answer to what makes a promotional merchandise item good is results-oriented thought. Thought, planning, and understanding not just of your market, but of promotional items themselves, most often produces good promotional merchandise programs.

Managers who are encouraged to think about every aspect of their own product line tend to venture into the promotional merchandise medium with the same thought process. These managers, and the companies they work for, realize that good promotional items are not just bought, they are thought out. The proof of this thought process is when merchandise naturally ties into overall corporate communications objectives as well as specific departmental objectives such as increased sales, marketing changes, personnel recognition, productivity and motivation, quality control, or product advertising. The promotional materials have the correct level of visibility with the correct audience. They solicit and receive the endorsement of the recipient. They create a positive impression within the target audiences. Their message is memorable for as long as it is supposed to be memorable. They are cost effective. They are free of hazard: no chemicals leak out, no sharp edges protrude, no lead-based paint peels off.

RELATIVITY IS NOT THEORETICAL

Buried in the above platitudes is relativity. The relative nature of the successful promotional item means that what is good today or tomorrow for this event with this group of people probably will not work when even one variable is slightly changed. It is important to understand that nobody controls—or even knows—all the variables. (Why did Ollie North T-shirts fail while Spuds MacKenzie T-shirts succeeded?) Some people come pretty close, however, to understanding some of the forces that can affect a promotional merchandise program. (*Program* is a key word in this chapter. If you have not yet embraced the concept of a program as opposed to buying 144 hats for the sales meeting, this chapter will have little relevance.)

Moving from theory into corporate practice, BMW provides this chapter's main case history. There are others, including the original Ghostbusters promotional merchandise and a Philips Lighting case history, that show how a worldwide company with an unknown commodity helped solve its identity problems by using promotional merchandise. But a car company—BMW—was chosen as the lead topic for several reasons:

- Automobiles themselves could technically be defined as promotional merchandise. They solicit the endorsement of the user, project an image of the manufacturer whose logo appears on the product, identify the user as a member of a group, and provide the manufacturer with hundreds of millions of dollars of free, high-credibility advertising as owners drive them.
- It is the car companies, then, to no one's surprise, that have traditionally utilized and benefited from premiums and ad specialties. Some car companies have effectively integrated them into their product line.
- Because dealerships have parts departments, the pipeline to receive and the structure to inventory and sell merchandise at a reasonable price already is in place.
- But most of all, car companies and their dealers come as close to profitably preaching to the choir as any corporate group—their choir is their customer base of ready-to-buy enthusiasts.

WHY BMW?

The specific car company—BMW—was chosen for several reasons:

- The company sells cars as well as motorcycles. Two groups of promotional merchandise users can be studied within one company.
- The German-based manufacturer sells its products all over the world, and has a substantial history of communicating with virtually all management levels, departments, and end users through merchandise.
- BMW management is experimenting with scientific research to determine the effectiveness of its promotional merchandise programs.
- BMW appeals to a broad range of buyers, as well as non-buyers, with its autos and motorcycles. The company's 3 series autos are one of the largest selling models in its class in the world.
- BMW management isn't afraid to talk openly about what does and doesn't work.

COFFEE, TEA, OR GOGGLES

When you walk into a BMW showroom in Munich, West Germany, you could be greeted with a cup of coffee in a bright white porcelain mug that says in very small type in four languages, "Welcome to BMW." If, however, you happen by a dealership in the United States you may well find a white T-shirt with a logo as big as the size allows on display in a glass case near the parts window. Flipping through virtually any car or motorcycle magazine or any aftermarket parts catalog, you're likely to find a BMW something. Walk down a busy street in a tourist town, and you're likely to see unlicensed BMW paraphernalia being sold.

The person in charge of merchandise in the United States is Mr. Til Roemer, vice president of parts and accessories for BMW North America, Inc. A German who has lived in the United States for more than a decade, Mr. Roemer knows and states, "the U.S. is not one market. It is 20 or 30, at least. What is popular in one part of the country is not popular in another."

To illustrate his statement on a global level, he shows a page from a German edition of a BMW accessory catalog featuring goodies specifically for the 325i convertible.

"Would you wear this?" he asks, pointing to a woman wearing a leather form-fitting helmet with goggles and scarf, breezing along the road in a topless Bimmer.

"It's like the Red Baron," he says. "And, it is very popular in Germany."

His answer to the helmet and goggles question, for the 20 or 30 markets in the United States, is "no." People would not wear the soft leather helmet and goggles.

Then he turns and says, "Would you buy mud flaps for your BMW? They are very popular here in the U.S. with that big BMW logo on them."

And so it goes as Mr. Roemer pulls out catalog after catalog. One features Spring M-style sports clothes, another features clothes for winter. (M, which signifies Motorsport, is the high performance letter designation for limited production BMWs.) There is a $6,000 watch on one page of another catalog, a $7,000 set of custom trunk-fitted luggage for the flagship V-12 model 750iL on another page of a different catalog.

"We sell the luggage in Europe. In America, people who have enough money to buy the 750 will take a plane instead of driving, so they don't need our luggage. In Europe, they would be more likely to drive. Dealers buy the watch," he says, "for themselves."

RADIO CAP ON DIFFERENT WAVELENGTH

Then Mr. Roemer disappears for a minute. When he returns, he is holding a cheap baseball cap—royal blue polyester with the blue, white, and black BMW logo embroidered on a patch sewn on the cap front. The hat is gaudy, one of those that look better when they're dirty. The electric blue polyester fibers glisten even in the natural light coming in through the large windows of Mr. Roemer's Montvale, New Jersey, office. The patch—which could not be any bigger and still fit on the front of the hat—turns the refined German motorcar and motorcycle logo into the equivalent of a hand-lettered "For Sale by Owner" sign that might stand in the front lawn of a tract house.

But, it gets worse. The hat contains a radio. Cheap little ear plugs dangle from the sides of the cap. Metal eyelets in the bill act as wobbly anchors for the idle ear plugs. Very cheap little round knobs are sewn into the hat's right temple and a battery pocket takes up space on the left temple.

"They would go crazy if I sent these to Germany," Mr. Roemer says with a smile. "But if I sold these at a racetrack in the United States, I could sell every one I had."

SALES VERSUS CORPORATE IMAGE

Mr. Roemer then goes into a discussion of what will sell as opposed to what creates the desired image, as well as what is considered the proper BMW image in different countries throughout the world. The striking part of his verbal dissertation is that he doesn't look at the baseball cap-cum-radio with disdain (as many BMW owners would), but sees it as appealing to a market segment. It may not necessarily be the segment with which BMW North America has anything to discuss, but nevertheless Mr. Roemer's familiarity with product impact and its effect on image is without subjective judgment. His job is not to pick merchandise he likes, but to create and maintain the promotional merchandise program in the United States that achieves national, worldwide, and local dealer objectives.

Sometimes this includes trendy merchandise; but, as Mr. Roemer relates, these days the trendy stuff is passed over.

"We don't want to be known as a trendy company," he says, knowing full well that since 1986 the BMW has been undisputedly the trendiest car in the United States, Japan, and probably also in Great Britain and West Germany. The car has become the universal Yuppie badge—rolling proof of a good credit rating—and is the end-line of a thousand Yuppie jokes. (NBC's John Chancellor said in an editorial after the October 19, 1987, stock market crash, "The difference between a pigeon and a Yuppie is that at least a pigeon can still make a deposit on a BMW.")

To dilute this image and make room for others, BMW of North America no longer offers trendy clothes. The company previously introduced a spring and fall line with jackets, shirts, pants, headwear, and even footwear. BMW also offered ski wear, casual wear, some children's play clothes, and business attire. The products are still sold in other countries, but not in the United States.

"We did not sell a lot of our clothing in this country anyway," Mr. Roemer says. People don't walk into a BMW dealer to buy a necktie or a ski jacket. The clothing was strictly a customer-impulse buy, and people were not generally prepared to wait for the dealer to order their size. This meant the dealer had to keep several sizes of clothing in stock. With an average markup of only 35 percent, the items were not generating sufficient revenue before they went out of style.

"In addition," Mr. Roemer adds, "the items often cut into existing automobile sales profit. Many U.S. customers wanted things free. They felt if they were buying an expensive car, the dealer should give them something for nothing."

Add to these problems a high theft rate, and BMW management's awareness of the negative effects of being perceived as a trendy car company, and it's not difficult to understand why the seasonal clothes line was dropped in the United States. Still, the U.S. premium and ad specialty revenue exceeds $1.5 million a year; and while it is one of the best markets worldwide, Great Britain, Japan, and West Germany are strong promotional merchandise markets, too.

THE U.S./GERMAN DIFFERENCE: SEQUENTIAL PURCHASING

"In the United States, the bigger the logo, the better the sales. In Europe, the smaller the logo, the better the sales," Mr. Roemer says as he shows a several-hundred-dollar brown leather jacket that sells well in Europe and has a visually insignificant metal BMW moniker sewn into the waist.

But there are other differences between the U.S. and German merchandise, and these differences start with the way in which BMWs are purchased. Aside from the coffee in the BMW china mentioned earlier, customers in Germany and in many other parts of the world are able to customize their cars when they buy them. Major accessories, such as air conditioning, driving lights, and steering wheels, and minor ones like floor mats, a child's car seat, and a ski rack are all part of the buying decision in Europe. The showroom is arranged so that this sequential purchase of accessories comes naturally. Promotional merchandise is part of the accessory package and is displayed in the showroom along with the performance wheels and upgraded stereos. In the United States, BMW customers cannot make accessory decisions of any consequence. A U.S.-spec BMW is accessorized according to model before it leaves the factory. The U.S. version of sequential purchase action often takes place at the contract signing where buyers are verbally rubber-hosed into adding into the purchase price the cost of Teflon(TM) paint coating, chassis undercoating, alarms, removable radios, extended warranties, and other negative sell items. (Yes, whey you buy a BMW at some dealerships this can happen even though BMWs already have theft-proof radios, a state-of-the-art alarm system, and one of the best undercoating and paint protection systems that can be found on an automobile.) In this environment, it's no wonder that promotional merchandise does not fare well. Many dealer sales people see this not as an enjoyable consumer trip down accessory lane, but as an easy mugging in a dark alley; a salesperson's last chance to pick up lost profits from a sale where the buyer has wheedled and whined a way to a lower price. There is not a chance under these circumstances that a pleasant experience can be created whereby a customer might buy a couple of jackets and a Parker roller ball pen with the BMW logo on it. A salesperson would be a fool to try to sell a hat.

The customer is, however, ready to ask for the merchandise free on sight. This is why, in the United States, the merchandise is often hidden in the back next to the parts counter where it is almost inaccessible during the day, and totally inaccessible in the evening once the parts and service departments are closed.

PARTS & SERVICE, FRONT & CENTER

BMW's corporate policy is to have all aspects of the dealer's business in the showroom. This includes the parts counter, service desk, and accessory displays. BMW, however, does not control the actions of its dealers, and cannot force a dealer to remodel an existing facility. Although many U.S. car dealer principals lose consciousness at the thought of potential buyers rubbing shoulders with owners who are bringing their cars in for service, BMW believes its owner base is satisfied and encourages the mix of buyers and owners in the same room. Many salespeople would prefer not to have these two groups on the same planet. In instances where dealers have been convinced that BMW's policies are good for business, the closing rooms are closed and the parts counter and accessory case is brought out from the back.

EXAMINING THE ENVIRONMENT

This evolutionary refinement in automotive sales and service accepts as a premise that the customer will evolve, too. This means U.S. car buyers won't expect merchandise for free regardless of how many California car dealers walk across hoods with a tiger on a leash offering free T-shirts, floor mats, and air conditioning. In this environment, where the deal is paramount, selling the car takes all the effort a salesperson can muster. It is impossible to include the sales of promotional merchandise in the environment described above, unless they are used as a bribe. Not including these premiums in the selling environment, however, risks losing all the benefits of this sophisticated advertising medium. When you consider the level of sophistication in the television advertising campaign—the video equivalent of the missing link—of dealers like these, it is not hard to understand why there isn't much emphasis on promotional merchandise. These dealers know that they fail in this environment. Dealers may not realize why, but they see their job as selling cars, not deciphering the mysteries of giveaways. Creating the environmental integration of promotional merchandise is what is most remarkable about the BMW system. If premium and ad specialty textbooks existed, BMW's integration of promotional merchandise into diverse corporate policy areas that affect sales and customer satisfaction, employee morale and decor, quality and price, and centralized versus decentralized management would be a textbook example of a successful program. Promotional merchandise is part of the discussion in which showroom floor plans, car service, and customer showroom traffic patterns are discussed. Mr. Roemer (like many authoritative promotional merchandise managers interviewed for this book) understands the powerful nature of the medium and how to integrate it and its message into every cranny of the business.

This integration is most apparent in the motorcycle division. Motorcycle riders are better accessory consumers. They understand the value of accessories. Typical BMW motorcycle dealers will stock many sizes of jackets, full leathers, helmets, gloves, and even shoes and boots because they know their motorcycle customer is also their accessory/promotional merchandise customer.

Perhaps better known to Americans are the Harley-Davidson owners who sport the full color Harley logo across their weathered black leather jackets, inspiring reactions across a wide spectrum from nearly everyone.

Motorcycle buyers are not as likely to ask for the merchandise free as are car buyers, and they are more likely to make a specific trip to the dealership to purchase merchandise—unlike car customers.

Catalogs with motorcycle merchandise are usually well-done, full-color, professionally designed selling tools that find their way to the owners' home or office, and are promoted in enthusiast magazines and clubs.

FREE RIDERS

Many times, however, the merchandise advertised in publications or sold in public places is counterfeit.

"We try to keep the counterfeit merchandise off the market," Mr. Roemer says. "Our lawyers pursue the manufacturers, but we don't have much luck."

Mr. Roemer accurately describes the situation. On a test walk through New York City's Time Square and Theater District, BMW hats and T-shirts were available at nearly every souvenir stand. They were cheaply made and sold for around $6 for the shirt and $4 for the hat.

Nobody knows exactly what counterfeit promotional merchandise does to the image of the counterfeited company. It is a violation of U.S. law; it makes the counterfeiters a fair amount of money, but whether it encourages, discourages, or has no effect on the sale of BMW automobiles and motorcycles is anybody's guess.

There are several legal groups, funded by companies whose logos are continually knocked-off, that are hired to prosecute and research the situation, but these have met with limited success. City streets are full of illegal tennis shoe T-shirts, automobile hats, and Hard Rock Cafe clothing.

BMW has pulled from the market its own licensed line of clothing. There was for a short time a small shop in Beverly Hills that carried the BMW line; but, as Mr. Roemer says, "We're a car company, not a clothing retailer."

The retail operation was pursued as an advertising medium, not as a retail clothing division of BMW. Keeping up with styles and sizes, however, became too expensive compared with the resulting advertising produced by the clothing, so the operation was dropped.

"It didn't make sense at this time," Mr. Roemer says. "Maybe we'll do it again sometime, or in another country."

AFRAID OF NO GHOSTS

Accurately gauging what your market will accept is something a small advertising firm in New York City did correctly, and while this case history has nothing to do with BMW, it does show—as does the BMW case history—that management must stay close to the market it serves with promotional merchandise. Staying close means fine-tuning your current offering, as well as being able to read what your market will accept six months out.

The small New York agency that read its market was Ericksen/Basloe Advertising, an entertainment advertising and collateral agency. Their assignment was to promote the video tape version of *Ghostbusters*. What makes this case history interesting is that the year was 1981.

Think back to 1981. There weren't many VCRs, tape rental businesses, or tapes. Video tapes sold for $89.99 each. The great debate between Beta and VHS was raging, and nobody really knew which format would win out. The market was touted as enormous, but nobody had seen the millions in dollars that were talked of. Video tape companies were filling the pipeline with old movies because the gap between movie release and video release could be more than two years.

Ghostbusters was a phenomenally successful movie. The video tape version was brought out primarily for sale, not to rent; and the producers came to Bob Ericksen, a former publishing executive, and Steve Basloe, a former Columbia director of marketing and advertising.

The audience Ericksen/Basloe was assigned to was the video distributors—the group who would sell the tapes to the video dealers. Ericksen/Basloe had previously handled promotion duties for *The Big Chill* with 25,000 six-pack coolers to this same distributor group.

While theoretically, the agency's job was to move the tapes to the distributors, Ericksen/Basloe realized that promotional merchandise the distributors could either keep or pass on to the video dealers as an incentive to buy, probably would be more powerful and sell more tapes.

Their suggestion was a Ghostbuster telephone—an idea that would meet with groans and yawns today. But in 1981, it was the perfect incentive. Phone marketing was breaking out of the grips of the phone company thanks to Judge Harold Greene and his breakup decree. People were anxious to buy new phones. The Ghostbuster phone was more than just a Far East model with a logo imprinted on the handset. It was a slim, red, inexpensive, one-piece phone set into a hollow plastic Ghostbuster logo. The product was about a foot in diameter and could be hung on the wall or used on a desk.

This product, it turned out, had several useful lives. As a distributor incentive, it was an instant hit. The pass-through to the video dealers was nearly unanimous—once the distributor kept one for himself. The dealers displayed the phone providing additional advertising for a very popular and instantly recognizable logo.

Vice President Sara Basloe, sister of Steve, says that back then "This was not a measurable communication tactic. We knew the phone was successful because of demand for it and for the video. The movie was so successful and the song and the phrase were so well known that it was impossible to determine quantitatively how many additional video tapes distributors sold because they offered the phone. A distributor may carry 25,000 titles, and when he is writing an order, he will remember the phone and put down 10 copies of *Ghostbusters* instead of 5, because he knows he can qualify for another phone."

The phone was purchased in Hong Kong and the base was made in the United States. The total cost of the phone, base, shipping, assembly, and packing came to $9.00; $4.10 of this was for the phone.

DRIVING HOME GHOSTS

The common thread in these two case histories—BMW and *Ghostbusters*—is that management understands its market and understands how promotional merchandise will help reach its objectives. There is no argument over whether or not to use promotional merchandise, but how to use it. Maybe the results-oriented testing that can tie objective fulfillment directly to promotional merchandise is currently weak, but in both case histories, it is obvious that the correct application of promotional merchandise increases the chances of success. In the case of BMW, the results are long-term and dependent on many different factors, while the Ghostbusters incentive had a specific short-lived duty.

Steve Goldmacher, director of marketing communications for the consumer division of Philips Lighting, had an opposite problem from Ericksen/Basloe. While everyone knew *Ghostbusters,* Mr. Goldmacher worked for a Dutch company, known worldwide for its Norelco shavers, Magnavox televisions, Anchor Brush, and Philips audio and video systems, and not known well for its line of consumer light bulbs. Philips insured its number three position when it purchased the Westinghouse light bulb division, but still had an identity crisis.

A coordinated program of advertising, promotions, and sponsorship of the 1988 Seoul Olympics was constructed and promotional merchandise played—and continues to play—a pivotal role.

TRADING OLYMPIC PINS

When news of Olympic sponsorship came to Mr. Goldmacher, it was 1987, just before the Calgary games. The Dutch wanted to be sponsors in 1992, but they learned that if they did not get into the 88 games, they would not have the opportunity to get into the 92 games. The electronics category, which Philips wanted, was already taken by Panasonic, so Philips negotiated for lighting.

"We rushed to make the Calgary games," Mr. Goldmacher says, "and created an ad campaign—'We light the world for all the world to see.' Then," he says, "we developed merchandise to give to people who came to Calgary and Seoul—a package of tickets and, for Calgary, everything to keep you warm except long underwear. This included ski clothing, scarves, Thermos™ bottles, bags, ponchos, everything we could think of. When people arrived, they received the package. Everything had our logo on it."

The most demanded merchandise, however, was the Olympic pins. Mr. Goldmacher says, "the proximity of Calgary to the U.S., and the large number of U.S. suppliers and sponsors made for an unbelievable pin-trading atmosphere."

In Seoul, he explained, most people were buying pins. They felt it was property; but at Calgary, people went around with pins on their hat or vest, and other people would stop them to trade.

"In Calgary, we were still new at this, and we had a bland pin. The Europeans [Philips headquarters] were sponsors worldwide, so we took their pin and redesigned it. When we got to Calgary," he says, "we realized the pin wasn't good enough. It didn't have the proper documentation on the back because we hadn't used the official manufacturer or gotten Olympic Committee approvals. We learned fast, and for the Seoul games, we went to the official supplier (Ho Ho on New York's lower west side) and got official pins made."

The Olympic Games provided a substantial umbrella for promotions, and went a long way toward bringing the Philips name to light bulb consumers in the United States, but Mr. Goldmacher was charged with the nitty-gritty job of increasing sales, shelf space, and brand preference.

"In the light bulb business," he says, "there is no brand preference. When your bulb burns out, you buy another one. You don't necessarily look at who makes it."

Unless the company who makes it is offering a watch that is tied into a promotion for daylight savings time changes, and the ad says, "it's time to change your bulb." The "who" was Philips lighting, and the Philips division gave away 15,000 wrist watches—battery replaceable models—with the Philips Lighting logo on the face.

When it gets dark earlier, they reasoned people would be thinking of light bulbs. The promotion worked. To get the watch, a consumer purchased two flood lights and sent in proofs of purchase.

The watch was on stream with the trendy inexpensive fashion watches selling in department and specialty stores for around $30. Although this watch was nowhere near that price category, consumers understood its purpose, and it quickly became a campy must-have item.

PHIL WORKS FOR PHILIPS

With the daylight savings promotion under his belt, Mr. Goldmacher searched for another reason to remind consumers to buy Philips bulbs. He came up with one—Punxsutawney Phil. He purchased the rights to the legendary but fictitious ground hog from the Punxsutawney, Pennsylvania, Chamber of Commerce; changed the face a little; and planned its promotion. If Phil sees his shadow on Ground Hog Day, there will be six more weeks of winter—six more weeks of dark days. The Philips factory is making, as this book goes to press, light bulbs with a green, blue, or red Punxsutawney Phil shadow that will light up when they are turned on. If a consumer gets one of these bulbs, he or she wins a prize.

By the time you read this, you will know whether the program was a success. The top prize of $33,000 (Philips bulbs last 33 percent longer than the competition) was rounded out with other cash prizes and 1,500 Punxsutawney Phil coffee mugs.

"I CAN SING TOO, MR. BENNETT"

Mr. Goldmacher's creativity came from himself and his agency, Saatchi & Saatchi Worldwide. He looks at ad specialty and premium salespeople as vendors rather than partners or members of his creative team. "I want ad specialty people to know how to get merchandise at a good price and deliver it on time," he says.

Mr. Goldmacher has good reason not to expect creativity from his specialty advertising vendors. Mr. Goldmacher, however, never met Keith Smykal, now known as specialty advertising's singing ambassador (he has taken up his first love—singing—and is marketing it and his abilities as a lyricist to the corporate world for meetings and convention musicals). Mr. Smykal's creativity and inventiveness is almost unheard of in the specialty advertising industry. In 1952, Mr. Smykal was singing at the Waldorf Astoria Hotel in New York City when he met Liberace during a break. Mr. Smykal, during the day, was creating an ad specialty business that would make him a comfortable man financially, as well as provide a creative outlet. He presented Liberace with a sterling silver pin that had the pianist's famous piano sketch chemically etched on the face.

"Liberace bought 150 from me and it started my business," Mr. Smykal says.

But it didn't help his singing career. He became known in celebrity circles as the person who could create jewelry, and once—when delivering an order to Tony Bennett—he says (some

35 years later), "I wanted to say, 'I can sing, too, Mr. Bennett,' " but he didn't.

DUTCH BOY GIVES GROWN-UP ORDER

Mr. Smykal's jewelry prowess got him a 100,000-piece order for Dutch Boy(TM) paint tie tacks at $1 each. "We made a good profit on that order," he says smiling, "and it really got us rolling."

Rolling to Mr. Smykal was more than being a middleman. He sliced through the definition of agent, middleman, and supplier—buying raw materials and assembling them, engraving trophies, plaques and anything else he could get into his machines, and etching on sterling silver.

It was a trip to the offices of Mack Truck in the Empire State Building one day that paid off in 30 years of sales—well over $7 million.

"I showed the Mack buyer a little black case with my handmade jewelry samples, and four or five months later she called and said a national jewelry firm wouldn't sell her less than 100 of what she wanted, but she only needed 24. "I sold her 24," he says. In this case, what made the promotional item good was that there were only 24 of them.

But what made Mr. Smykal's merchandise different was that he was willing, in fact he preferred, to make custom merchandise. He didn't like relying on a catalog. "I used to walk up and down the streets of New York finding the people who could make plates and sew, make molds and do custom work," he says.

For his efforts, all of his products that have sold well have been custom made, beginning with the Dutch Boy(TM) tie tacks and including the famous news photo of Nancy Reagan using a phone with one of his gold, personalized receiver covers over it and the Mack Truck bulldog at one end. "We sold more than 250,000 of those covers, until," he says. "They started making so many different phones that we could not get one cover to fit them all."

ZIPPING UP AN ORDER

Talon Inc., the zipper manufacturer, "always wanted something different and distinctive." One year Mr. Smykal designed for the company a gold-plated cocktail stirrer with a zipper handle. "They loved it," he says. He followed this with product after product that used the Talon™ zipper or showed it in a different way.

All the time, Mr. Smykal didn't consider himself an ad specialty salesman. "I do more than sell ad specialties," he says today, with seven Clios to his credit and a philosophy that "makes me feel like I've just been riding along these last 35 years." His ride, though, has crystallized his feeling about his industry.

"There is no worse purchase than a cheap key chain," he says. "If you buy 5,000 for 25-cents each, you've spent $1,250. Nobody wants to use a cheap key chain, and although they may take them, they throw them away. If 10 get used," he says, exaggerating to make his point, "you've spent $125 per 'cheap' key tag." His point is not lost on his customers, however, especially Mack Trucks, Inc., which has been distributing his high-quality chrome ashtrays with the actual bulldog hood ornament on them for the last 20 years. (Mr. Smykal receives the bulldogs from the official supplier and modifies them in his Long Branch, New Jersey shop to fit on the ashtray.)

PULLING A HAT OUT OF A RABBIT

This was the theme of a Volkswagen campaign Mr. Smykal dreamed up himself and then sold to Volkswagen of America. The dealer promotion involved a hat Mr. Smykal designed and made, which was placed in the back of a Volkswagen Rabbit. "People would come into the showroom and pull a hat out of the rabbit," he says with a smile.

Did he win a Clio for this? "No, I didn't. I won one for the Pan Am commemorative plates, though," he says. "It's funny," he continues. "One day I was looking for the Clios and I couldn't find all of them. One of my salesmen had sold two of them as trophies. I think he got $35 a piece for them," he says laughing.

BACK TO SCHOOL

Not all of Mr. Smykal's ideas are successful with the right people. Disturbed by what he saw as a need for school children to be encouraged to accept responsibility for their own behavior, he began, unilaterally, the I Can Manage Myself Club for grades kindergarten through 5 at Gregory School in Long Branch, New Jersey. The objective of the promotional merchandise program was to teach children to listen attentively, work independently, and follow school rules.

While talking about the program, Mr. Smykal brings out a brown loose leaf binder that explains in detail the Teacher/Pupil Motivational Program. First, membership cards were issued to all students. Then came the decals with the special program logo. Then a photo cube that holds pencils and a pen light. "This was the first time most of these children had their own flashlight," he says. Then a Mr. Gregory bank that separates quarters, nickels, dimes, and pennies.

Mayor Philip D. Huhn wrote each student a letter, and when Mr. Smykal did follow-up research, he found that 80 percent of the 375 children who participated in the program regarded themselves as achievers and as members of the I Can Manage Myself Club.

Mrs. Munson, a fourth-grade teacher, said in a letter Mr. Smykal used as a testimonial, "My first impression of the program was that it was going to be a lot more paperwork, and I guess I was a little bit annoyed at the thought that there was another set of cards, papers and charts to be kept, but I found that it was really very little trouble to maintain and that the overall improvement in behavior was worth it." Mrs. Ware, a first-grade teacher said, "The overall improvement, I think, was the fact that the school pride was heightened, it really was, and I think that's a fantastic thing. The feeling of self-worth with the children was heightened."

Mr. Smykal paid all the costs of the program for the first year. He asked the school officials to help defray costs for the second year and they refused. The program died, but not Mr. Smykal's enthusiasm for it. He still has hope that someone will help finance a good promotional merchandise program like this that helps motivate grade school children who might otherwise miss the opportunity.

CHAPTER 3

APPLYING DIME STORE PSYCHOLOGY TO 25-CENT GIVEAWAYS: STUDYING YOUR AUDIENCE

Getting something for nothing—or at least without paying for it—is probably the best reason people like promotional merchandise so much. But this explanation doesn't address the questions of why people keep and treasure it; why people will allow themselves to be motivated beyond their normal productivity in order to take possession of it; why people will buy and steal it.

There is something else going on here, and if you—the buyer—understand the psychology of promotional merchandise and why people love it, you're more likely to have a successful promotional merchandise program. There are several concepts—such as perceived value, benefit, peer pressure, and membership in a select group—which contribute to making a promotional merchandise program successful. But you can't always control these factors. You, the buyer, have to create the environment in which these concepts can work so your promotional merchandise program is successful. If you start to dissect the process too much, you'll start asking yourself questions that have no answers. Some questions, however, can and must be answered to create this successful environment.

TAKE A CHANCE

There is always the chance that what you think is the perfect merchandise, will be—that without any thought, research, preparation, conversation or study, you will hit upon the end-all promotional merchandise that people will kill and die for. It has happened. Without so much as an internal memo or a meeting, promotional merchandise has been bought and distributed, and the campaign has made its buyer a star. Congratulations if you are one of those buyers who has experienced the promotional merchandise equivalent of winning the lottery. Skip the questions below and continue following your hunches.

If you haven't yet won the promotional merchandise lottery, you might want to consider applying the answers from the following questions to your next promotional merchandise purchase. It could increase the odds of your particular giveaway, geegaw, gift, or gimmick doing the communications job you want it to do.

KNOW YOUR AUDIENCE

If you don't know your audience, your promotional merchandise won't work. If you do know your audience, understand that this group of people does not know what it wants—only what it doesn't want—so don't let your audience pick its own merchandise.

You must read your audience's mind and determine what promotional merchandise is best. This isn't as difficult as it may seem. The following questions will help clarify the gray areas of your audience's gray matter.

There is one caveat, however: Because you are dealing with a group, it is impossible to answer the following questions about your audience with absolutes. At this point in your promotional merchandise research, you are seeking general information about the target group and yourself, not specific information about each person in that group, so general answers will lead you in the right direction.

INTERPRETING THE DATA

Once you have answered the questions, it is in the interpretation—the application of the dime-store psychology you will learn here—that you are most likely to err or succeed. Give yourself plenty of interpretative leeway, and don't assume that your interpretations are correct until you discuss them with someone else.

AUDIENCE TEST

1. What Is the Average Age of Your Audience?

Anyone who has a teenager or a two-year-old child knows there is a generation gap. Ignore this most basic audience demographic, and you will be doing the promotional merchandise equivalent of the Lucky Lindy while your audience is dancing the tango—with your competitor. Many promotional merchandise buyers naturally think of themselves when they purchase merchandise. If you, the buyer, are a middle-aged paint-by-numbers aficionado, the door prize at the company picnic or the trade show is likely to be the 16 by 20, 200-color snow-on-the-mountain scene. If on the other hand, you are the resident 23-year-old jogging addict, your idea of soul music is likely to be the scruff of worn running shoes on asphalt. With you in charge, everyone is likely to be presented with matching sweat bands—head and wrist.

So once you have identified at which generation you are aiming your promotional merchandise, identify to which generation you belong. Mentally chart the distance between the two and honestly decide whether you have the mental stretch to choose promotional merchandise that will cross the gap in the generations. Try to ignore what you think is a great item—even if you are in the generation of the target audience—unless that item fulfills your communications objectives.

Aging the Promotional Merchandise

Here are a few product/age group insights to get you started in the right interpretive direction. Once you see how the logic works, you can apply it to products you are considering for your promotional merchandise program:

The most common promotional merchandise is the pen. Everyone likes expensive pens, but older audiences tend to respect and take care of them more than younger audiences. If you buy an expensive pen for a young audience—anyone under 35—they probably won't appreciate it as much as someone over 35. On the other hand, business people over 35 probably have a lot of pens. If your audience is used to getting expensive pens (or the inexpensive models of pens with expensive-sounding names such as Cross and Tiffany), they may not appreciate it as much as if you gave something else.

If you decide on a pen, its cost and brand name should be determined by the assumed reactions of the recipients, not by your often arbitrary promotional merchandise budget or personal taste. If you decide your audience demands more pen than you have budget, don't buy a pen. Slapping a logo on a Bic pen and giving it to a Parker audience is throwing away money and positive image. Conversely, if you have the budget for a pen that you think matches your audience's expectations, it doesn't necessarily mean a pen is the best promotional merchandise. In addition to fulfilling the psychological criteria, there are other criteria detailed elsewhere in the book that make a successful product.

Golf Balls—Possibly the Worst

Golf balls sporting a company logo have a narrow appeal, even in the most sporting of companies, and even among avid golfers. There are several reasons why golf balls can be wrong, and age can be a determining factor. If the golfers are young and poor, they will appreciate a golf ball. They won't complain if it is not their brand, or the brand they would like to be able to afford. If, however, the golfers are a bit wealthier and it isn't their brand, they will most likely accept the golf ball, but it will be the one they use last—only when they have to. If they transfer this thought to your company's product line, that probably isn't the communications objective you're seeking. This is why the worst promotional merchandise to give a group of middle-aged golfers can be a golf ball. Close your eyes and imagine 50 golfers opening packages of golf balls with your two-color logo emblazoned on the dimples. What do you hear as they talk to each other? "It's not my brand." Those are death words to a product manager, and to risk mixing them with a promotional merchandise message is communications suicide.

But there is one more reason why golf balls may be the worst item to give away. Price. As any golfer knows, sporting goods stores make little or no profit on golf balls. Pro shops make a bit more, but ordinarily golf balls are the loss leaders. Imprinted golf balls, however, are sold at retail prices (even to the ad specialty middlemen who are supposed to get better prices) with very little discount for quantity considerations, and there are extra charges for the imprinting. It is not difficult to find the same golf balls you bought for $26 to $30 a dozen with your logo on them to be selling for half that without your logo at the discount sporting goods store. The recipient's perceived value of the golf balls is $13 a dozen, not the $26 or $30 you paid. This perceived value disparity alone is often enough evidence to keep promotional merchandise buyers away from golf balls.

Wearables Might Wear Well

Baseball caps usually are favored by young men, bald men (keeps their heads warm in winter, shaded in summer), and children—not women of any generation. Visors have serious appeal to many women—visors co-exist peacefully with hair styles and look sporty without being masculine.

Other products are age indifferent, such as coffee mugs or other glassware, T-shirts, calculators, and calendar and appointment books. Some items, however, may have immediate appeal, but won't be used by certain audiences; therefore, generally it's not a good idea to ask your audience what it wants. Such items include belt buckles. Nearly every male will express interest in having a good-looking belt buckle, but only a narrow group of males actually will wear the buckle. The rest will keep it in their desk drawer, give it to their children or take it home and save it. Any promotional merchandise that people want to take home and save is suspect, since it probably won't be doing its communications job tucked away in the user's bureau drawer.

You Add the Realism

The problem with these kinds of generalizations is that while they can lead you in the right direction, they can be full of holes, too. Among the audience you want to reach, you may know that the golfers only use a certain brand of ball. You buy that brand and you are a hero. Maybe you want your audience to take your merchandise home and save it—a personal heirloom from your company. Only you can be specific enough about your audience's generation to make a sensible promotional merchandise decision that combines your distinct knowledge with your ability to glean additional insights.

One way to increase the odds of making the right decision once you know which generation you are targeting is to go where that generation goes during its leisure time. This is where your audience will most honestly display its likes and dislikes. If you want to understand what influences the purchasing decisions of senior citizens, go to a mall on a weekday morning. If you want to see how teens act, go just about anywhere in the evening. If you want to see how boaters, skiers, or rabbis act—go where they go.

Observation is a powerful tool in audience interpretation, and the more accurately you fulfill the needs and wants of your audience, the more successful your promotional merchandise program will be.

2. Is Your Audience Comprised of Conspicuous Consumers?

While you're watching your audience, see how conspicuous their purchases are. Questions three and four will help define this habit more, but to answer this question look for items like big jewelry, flashy watches, argyle socks, earrings (on men and women), $100 tennis shoes, or $700 hand-made shoes. Also, notice the inconspicuous consumers. Maybe your audience is made up of people who wear custom-made clothes that look just a little rumpled or leather shoes with chamois linings. Careful observation will lead to accurate mind reading and the right choice of merchandise. Don't necessarily be fooled into thinking that a quiet, inconspicuous consumer will not wear your logo conspicuously across his or her chest. Other factors come into play when the recipient makes the decision whether or not to prominently display your message. The conspicuous consumer may settle for a cheaper version of the merchandise, or he or she may demand a designer version with the designer label as evident as your logo.

3. What Kind of Clothes Do They Wear?

Nothing tells more about a person's value system in the circumstances you are working under than dress. Regional customs and costumes aside, the obvious observations are simple and straightforward when it comes to determining which people would be attracted to which promotional merchandise. Don't offer a steam iron as an incentive to a man who wears wrinkled shirts to work. Likewise, don't offer designer accessories to women who wear no-nonsense clothes. An expensive leather brief case is lost on a person who is happy with a canvas bag or a big yellow envelope. And even if the intended recipients use a briefcase they may be reluctant to give up the current one. People get attached to things like briefcases. Your bright-idea briefcase may sit in a closet for years, not pressed into service until a distant relative gets married or his son needs a wedding gift. On the other hand, a quality umbrella in the right climates, is in demand regardless of the polyester content in the wardrobe or whether the employee or customer sports a white or blue collar. (Please note the word *quality* is used to describe the umbrella.)

Uniforms Don't Always Signal Uniformity

If your audience wears uniforms, there are several conclusions you can draw. They are intimately familiar with group behavior, and they naturally tend to gravitate toward group activities. Unlike the Beverly Hills debutantes, audiences who wear uniforms have no aversion to showing up in the same outfit for the social event of the year. Use this uniformity to your advantage when you buy merchandise for this audience. They won't mind a bit showing off your logo when it signifies their membership in your group. Structured recognition in the form of stepped design often works well when you want to recognize individuals or subgroups. This can be accomplished with gold embroidery instead of company colors, scrambled eggs on the baseball caps for the upper echelon group members, or other upgrades of the same basic merchandise. If you can extend the uniform through promotional merchandise, often members of this group will help pay for the merchandise. For example, you can offer writing instruments or upgraded working tools with logos. The key here is that your audience of uniform wearers is comfortable promoting an ideology, a value system, and even a product. You can take advantage of this tendency to advertise and encourage them to use it to your advantage.

One last advisory: If your audience is in the clothing business, stay away from a wearable item. You're likely to be faced with recipients who either could have bought it wholesale, know it is last year's style (as most promotional merchandise wearables are), or is so immune to clothing that nothing wearable motivates them.

4. What Kind of Car Do They Drive?

Except in New York City, the kind of car your audience drives could be all you need to know to give them the right merchandise. Make sure, however, the kind of car your audience drives is the kind of car they want to drive. For example, if your audience is made up of men and women in their late forties to mid-fifties driving four-year-old sedans, and they are solid middle and upper middle income people, find out if they have kids in college. The old man might want a Cadillac Allanté but he's college-poor and Hyundai-ridden at the moment.

Rather than basing your research on the amount of money your audience spends on a car, look at what type of automobile they drive. If the audience parking lot is a sea of econo-boxes, you have people who fly on their vacations, look at autos as transportation, and probably take what they consider to be a sensible approach to expenses—they're cheap. These are the people who will take five T-shirts, all in different sizes, for their family members because it means they won't have to buy them for the kids when school starts. If you were counting on your T-shirts being worn in the near future, you could be mistaken if you give them to this kind of audience. If, however, you want to help clothe the children without embarrassing the recipients, buy a lot of kid's sizes, and you've reached your goal. Econo-box drivers appreciate and remember that you T-shirted their family. A situation similar to T-shirting a family exists at Ingersoll-Rand Company headquarters in Woodcliff Lake, New Jersey. Instead of giving away T-shirts, however, apples are the merchandise. The company owns an apple orchard adjacent to the headquarters building and offers the crop free each season to employees who go out and pick the fruit. It is a nice gesture, and could easily be considered a promotional merchandise directed to employees to boost morale and keep them healthy.

Fulfilling Fantasies

If you see a covey of BMWs, Mercedes, and Porsches you can figure your audience is in debt in a big way, but they are having fun fulfilling their automotive fantasies. They will take four T-shirts for themselves, and they will wear them as long as the logo coincides with their value system.

Aging Plymouth Dusters, new Pontiac Trans Ams, Camaros, and other, fat-tired, loud-stereoed performance cars belong to yet another subgroup who, like their more expensive car counterparts, are living their four-wheeled fantasies. This group, however, often appreciates the less subtle promotional merchandise. When you're deciding on how large an imprint to put on the back of the jacket, make it bigger. This group will take two sets of anything and share it with a boyfriend or girlfriend. If it will hang from the rear view mirror, it will appeal to this group. Anything that hangs on the windows with suctions cups is an immediate hit. If it is offensive to 85 percent of the population, has a not-so-subtle sexual meaning, or if the kids can play with it while they are in the car, it also probably will be a hit with this group.

Tail-Wind Toilers

Suppose you look out and see the glistening chrome of bicycles? Find out first if the riders are happy bicyclists or unhappy pedalers. There is a group of healthy people who wear their health on their sleeves and their little rear-view mirrors on their glasses frames. They believe everyone should ride a bike to work, run, and eat healthy foods. They are angry at those who don't agree with them. The perfect promotional merchandise for this kind of personality is one that declares to the world the righteousness of the position. What they would really like is something that they could aim at car tires that would make them go flat, but they will be happy with something that makes them feel healthy.

The bike riders who ride because they like it (recognizable because they are not as thin as their tires and they don't wear $100 bicycle shoes) are in the mainstream and are receptive to products that make their riding more enjoyable. Because bicyclists are used to being forgotten as they ride with the four wheeled vehicles, promotional merchandise that recognizes their status as two-wheelers can make a positive impression.

No Car

Big city commuters often don't drive so it may not be possible to determine what kind of car someone has. They may take a subway to work, not own a car, and rent a Ferrari on the weekends. If a city person is driven, and the company isn't paying, that person falls into the conspicuous consumer category, unless they are busy people who work in the backseat of the car on their way to somewhere else. It's advisable not to weigh this question too much if you're not at an office building with a parking lot.

5. What Is the Average Education?

Probably nothing except super-wealth divides America like education. The difference between drop-out, high school graduate, college graduate, and higher is normally to the bone. In this category, more than any other, too, it is especially difficult for the promotional merchandise buyer to understand the motivations of audiences who do not share his educational experiences. Typically, a buyer with a college education, when faced with the task of buying promotional merchandise for a street fair that will be attended by non-college-educated people, will buy condescendingly. This buyer will drag out the cheap T-shirts, the bottle openers, the balloons. That same buyer, purchasing for a tennis tournament will purchase more expensive T-shirts, visors, or upscale key tags. The question you need to answer is whether this separation based on education needs to be made. Can you achieve the same success level with each group even though you spend less on one group than the other? If you can, you would be wasting company money if you didn't spend less. If you spend less and are perceived as cheap, you also will have wasted your promotional merchandise budget.

Trends Are Education-Specific

College-educated buyers will be more familiar with trendy products of their social group, so when these buyers must purchase for a less-educated group, they may not be successful spotting trends or fads unique to the audience that could enhance the corporate communications message. The other end of this discussion puts the grizzled company purchasing agent who is used to hammering out deals with Willie Loman salesmen in the uncomfortable position of buying something for the accounting department annual party. Cheap usually reigns and everybody jokes.

One way to counteract a very natural tendency to buy at your own education-taste level is to be aware that there are other levels—above and below yours—and not to go with your first idea of the perfect product.

Dollars and Books

It is also critical not to confuse education and economics. Poor people are not necessarily stupid, and wealthy people are not necessarily smart. If you are buying for people who are not college graduates, do not assume that they view themselves as undereducated or poor, even though you may. If your audience is undereducated and poor, don't buy them something cheap. Nobody knows—or hates—cheap things more than a poor person.

6. Who Is Your Audience and How Loyal Are They?

Once you determine who you are dealing with, you can begin to learn how loyal they are or are likely to become. Here, common sense makes the most sense. If your audience is made up of loyal customers and they happen to be in the arms of a competitor, learn all you can about them and make the up-front investment to woo them over. Woo doesn't mean bribe. It means integrate your promotional merchandise into your sales and marketing plan so that the competitor's customer is persuaded to use your product or service. An interesting example of this concept was implemented at Dr Pepper Corporation. With lagging vending machine sales, the company put a Dr Pepper™ T-shirt instead of soda in random cans. An advertising campaign alerted consumers that when they purchased Dr Pepper™ from a vending machine, they might instead get a more valuable T-shirt. Dr Pepper™ vending machine sales shot up, and sales continued at elevated levels after the promotion. Dr Pepper knew that soft drink customers could be loyal, so it made the up-front investment to woo them over.

Suppose, however, your customers are not loyal? Suppose they wander from brand to brand? It would seem, then that the best item would be a cheap one that induces them to buy immediately. The cereal companies have turned this tactic into a science with fraction-of-a-cent geegaws inside the box.

Tread Lightly with Employees

Employees can be your audience, and they too can be loyal or not. While many of the same marketing rules apply, other more complex notions of family and responsibility come into play when you are considering promotional merchandise for this group. The possibility of a negative reaction is much greater when the audience is employees than when it is customers or the general public. Employees demand more from promotional merchandise, and the buyer who does not take into account the grouse factor is underestimating the negative power of the item and probably overestimating its positive effect.

For example, many employees get office supplies free—they steal them from the company. A desk-oriented gift that is little better than something they could steal will have a negative effect. Cost, too, plays a powerful, negative role. Many employees will add up the cost of the 2,000 caps, or the sports team uniforms and declare that if the money were used for raises, everyone could be living better. Again, to ignore these negatives when purchasing promotional merchandise is foolhardy. To avoid most of the negative reactions, study the audience without assuming that you already know them. If employees receive something they worked for, it will be more valuable. To be successful, it must be equal to or better than the quality of the product that employee produces. If your company manufactures high-quality goods, it cannot give low-quality promotional merchandise to employees. This mixed message will confuse workers and probably elicit rude comments about the promotional merchandise you thought would produce a good feeling.

7. How Much Money Would Each Member of Your Audience Spend on Vacation? More or Less than You Would?

The purpose of this question is to give you a dollar orientation for budgeting purposes. You know how well you do or don't live and how much you spend on vacation versus how much you would like to spend. If you can approximate the same habits in your audience, you will know how much a dollar is worth to them. For example, if your audience spends $500 a day on vacation, they will not be familiar with the customs and lifestyle of someone who spends $50 a day. Conversely, if your audience spends $50 a day on vacation, they are familiar with customs and lifestyles that would be utterly foreign to the $500-a-day vacationer. Do not use this question to make material judgements about your audience. Spending $50 a day on vacation does not necessarily make them cheap or poor. It reflects a priority that needs to be considered when compiling the dime-store psychological profile of the promotional merchandise recipient.

Answering these questions also allows you, the buyer, to see just how close you are to your audience. If you are likely never to see your audience on vacation, be aware that your lifestyle and value system may be so different that you will be unable, without serious consideration, to choose an appropriate item.

8. Does Your Audience Have Any Reason to Harbor Negative Feelings toward Your Company or Product?

The reason for this question is to determine whether you are dead in the water before you start. If the majority of your audience feels strongly negative about your company, either forego the promotional merchandise or use the opportunity to implement a promotional merchandise-based morale program to change their minds. If your audience consists of restless employees, don't mistakenly give them something thinking it will calm the restlessness. It won't. It often gets worse. Now they have something to gripe about. Address the reason for the restlessness. If promotional merchandise will help solve the problem, then use it. If the problem is that management has asked them to take wage cuts the last five years while executives have awarded themselves bonuses that make the pages of *Fortune Magazine,* a token gift will not solve the problem. Save the money; the extra profit generated can go toward your bonus.

9. Would the Average Person on the Street Be Familiar with Your Company Name and Logo?

Public recognition generally has a positive effect on a promotional merchandise program. Jackets that say "Late Night With David Letterman" on the back, or "Hard Rock Cafe" have a higher perceived value than those with "Pete & Al's Plumbing"—even to Pete and Al. If your company name or product is publicly recognized, your promotional merchandise has an inbred advantage. If nobody has heard of you, it's an uphill identity climb. Everyone likes to belong to a group that others recognize. The more exclusive the group and the more famous the name, the more people enjoy being in it. Promotional merchandise that identifies the user as a member of a network sports or newscrew is always in demand.

The point here is don't compete with the Hard Rock Cafe. If nobody knows your company, don't give away jackets with the company name on the back and expect the resulting advertising to increase sales. There are better ways to reach your audience. Look at the objective you want to reach with the merchandise. If you need a warm-up jacket for the company sports team, put the name of the team, the recipient's name and then the company name on the jacket. It will mean more to the recipient. Or, co-op a jacket with Hard Rock Cafe, Coca-Cola, Walt Disney, Wheaties, or any other well-known brand or company. Often these companies jump at the chance to share the spotlight in a targeted market segment like your employees or customers. The benefit to you is that your audience wearing your jacket now belong to two exclusive groups—your company which nobody knows, and the co-oping company which everyone knows.

10. If They Knew They Wouldn't Be Caught, Would This Audience Steal the Merchandise You Chose because It Has Your Company's Logo on It?

This is a crass way of determining whether your company's logo makes the merchandise more or less valuable. The theft quotient and the merchandise cost can help determine how much you will have to spend to reach your audience and fulfill your communications objectives. To a child, the value of an eraser is incalculable when a Smurf is on it. The same eraser with the logo of a big eight accounting firm probably wouldn't appeal even to the most loyal employee of the firm.

Sometimes you can get a better understanding of theft quotient when you examine your company's own product line. If your audience needs what your company supplies, it won't generally want your promotional merchandise as much as if your audience wants what your company supplies.

CAN'T GIVE IT AWAY

Put another way, if you are the promotional merchandise buyer for a national franchised real estate company, your audience—real estate buyers and sellers—will tend to resist your promotional merchandise; that is, they won't steal it. One reason is because they don't want your basic services, they need them. Your product—real estate brokerage—is not perceived as sexy, romantic, or exciting. In fact, there are few buyers or sellers who would pass up the opportunity to bypass a real estate agent. A buyers' or sellers' reaction to your promotional merchandise could easily be that it is junk that might better be done away with so the agent's commission structure could be modified downward. In this case, your audience does not see its role as your advertising vehicle, and when it does, it generally resists that role.

The recipients of your real estate company's promotional merchandise are not likely to show it off, to display it as evidence of membership in a select club or to think fondly of your company while they use your giveaway gimmick.

It is up to you to get the promotional merchandise into your audience's hands and minds so that when they do need your company, they will call you, not your competitor. This can get expensive. The merchandise can be just as effective at reaching your communications goals as long as you make the distinction between promotional merchandise carrying a logo people want to display versus one they might resist using. Once you have determined this, you have determined whether or not your merchandise will be stolen.

STEAL IT FOR FREE

If you decide that your merchandise would be stolen based on the logo, make it freely available only to the audience you want to reach. Let the rest of the world wish it could have one of your geegaws. Put two locks on the promotional merchandise cabinet, tell everyone what is behind those locks, and give keys to people to whom you owe a power favor. This will make your audience—recipients of your largesse—loyal advertisers of your product as well as members in your select club. You will have paid off a debt to the key holders and made them members of an even more select group.

If you combine an audience of conspicuous consumers who have a propensity to steal your merchandise, you can perpetuate a very powerful communications program just letting these people steal their way to your objectives.

THEATRICAL RECOGNITION

Broadway and television show satin jackets fit into this category of eminently valuable merchandise in the hands of conspicuous consumers. These jackets have the show name and graphics embroidered on the back, and they are generally given only to the cast and crew. A person wearing one is an attention-getter, and the show benefits from the advertising. Evidence of the demand for this type of merchandise was clear when NBC opened a small shop on the ground floor of 30 Rockefeller Plaza in New York selling only merchandise with show logos. The tiny little alcove, tucked away in what should be a low traffic area, has one of the highest dollar per square foot volumes of any shop at 30 Rock.

GOLD MINE OR LAND MINE?

In the automobile aftermarket this geegaw larceny phenomenon is particularly evident, and can extend to economically insignificant items such as decals. Aftermarket luxuries such as expensive radios, high performance mufflers, cams, spoilers, and tires are promotional merchandise gold mines. Necessities such as lubricants and bolts, starter motors and clutches are promotional merchandise land-mines. The romance of the product sell is one factor that makes these premium automotive aftermarket products suitable with promotional merchandise. Another is their cost-visibility ratio. When motorists buy an expensive automotive component that nobody can see, the next best way to tell the world is with promotional merchandise. As the promotional merchandise buyer for a company like one described here, you might not care whether the promotional merchandise went to actual buyers or not. The primary emphasis in this case would be on the promotional merchandise recipient's ability to advertise your product to the right audience and generate more sales.

LOGO MAGIC CAN BE HAD

The only way to fail the test above is to fail to consider the answers to your questions.

When you do your homework and apply your dime-store psychology before buying your merchandise, your audience will experience the magic of the merchandise.

There is magic between the time when the baseball caps are hoisted off the ship from Taiwan and when they end up on the heads of the recipients with your logo embroidered on the front. But it only happens when you have the right information and can pull the right rabbit out of your own hat.

This magic can work for you or against you, and understanding the basic as well as the specific motivating factors related to the acquisition and display of promotional merchandise by the recipients can determine whether your magic is black or your magic is music.

CHAPTER 4

"IF I ONLY HAD A HEART": THE GEEGAW YOU WANT MAY ALREADY EXIST

This famous wish from the movie version of *The Wizard Of Oz* is fulfilled when the Wizard tells the Tin Man he already has a heart. Drawing on his own Zen Ozian philosophy, the Wizard explains that what the Tin Man thought he wanted, he already had. He just didn't know it.

The Wizard should be at promotional merchandise meetings imparting the same wisdom to buyers who are whining for something new. The misguided search for the new and different item seems never to stop—not even with two-billed baseball caps.

This chapter will try to convince you, the buyer, that you do not need to consider something new for your promotional merchandise program to be a success. It will further show that you will want to stay as far away from "somethings new" as you can.

LOGIC FAULT NUMBER ONE

The logic fault that creates the desire for new promotional merchandise items begins with the assumption that a never-before-seen gimmick will help make your program successful. What a never-before-seen gimmick in fact will do, if you buy it, is help make the gimmick successful.

SUBTRACTS POWER

The second logic fault is the assumption that the excitement generated by a new promotional merchandise item will flow to your product or message and increase its power. It is not logical to assume an automatic energy transfer to your product will take place.

Something new is more likely to subtract power from your message because it shares, and often steals, the communications spotlight. It diverts your audience's attention, encouraging discussion of the new product. Every second spent marveling at or griping about this new geegaw is a second not spent hearing and acting on your communications message.

Whenever your target audience receives your promotional merchandise, their perceptions of your company are transferred to the merchandise and vice versa. For example, if someone digs through the cereal box to get the plastic prize, existing audience perceptions already have ruled out attributes such as quality, long life, precision craftsmanship, or usefulness. Instead, the recipient knows he or she will get a minute of diversion while the giveaway is assembled (or identified), and a minute of use. After two minutes, the item will spend eternity at a local landfill. The merchandise has done its job, however. If you or your children rooted through the box to get the giveaway, it is reasonable to assume that the giveaway had some influence in the decision to purchase the cereal.

When you are a member of a target audience of scotch drinkers and Cutty Sark offers premiums you must purchase, you will expect and receive quality, usefulness, and a measure of status and prestige. You will expect the merchandise to be functional and have an acceptable life span.

Although you may be open to a wide variety of products, they all must fulfill your expectations and be in agreement with your perceptions. If your perceptions are not fulfilled—whether you are a member of the cereal or the scotch audience—you will have a negative reaction to the promotional merchandise and to the communications message.

Barnum, Come Here, I Need You

An example of mismatched perceptions occurred just after the breakup of the Bell System. Telephone manufacturers flooded the market with all shapes and qualities of phones. And, a lot of people who bought ridiculously low-priced phones proved P. T. Barnum's sucker-a-minute theory.

Many promotional merchandise buyers, realizing the high perceived value of a telephone (which the Bell System had cultivated for more than 100 years since Alexander Graham said "Watson, come here, I need you") offered cheap phones in promotional merchandise programs. For subscribing to a magazine or a service, or buying just a few dollars worth of goods, target audiences received a free phone. "What a deal," people thought. As visions of Western Electric quality danced in their heads, they rushed to dial the 800 number to order.

It didn't take long for recipients to realize that their perceptions had been toyed with. The cord often was so short they had to sit on the floor to use the phone, and the quality of the phone was barely measurable against cans and string. AT&T, not oblivious to the quality chasm, produced a series of commercials humorously reinforcing what some people learned the hard way—there is a difference in telephones.

Embracing Cheap and New

From a budget standpoint, you as the buyer, have to decide whether toying with people's perceptions is profitable. If it is, you will be doing your management and stockholders a favor by pursuing new merchandise like cheap phones, cheap clock radios, and cheap solar calculators. The knock-off world could be yours. Usually audiences with short memories handle cheap merchandise best. If you need to talk to your audience once a year or so, they may have forgotten that your phone didn't work or that the radio sounded like mission control. If you can come up with another new high-perception-low-quality product the next time you need to sell to your audience, they probably will buy again.

If a company is committed to new and cheap for the long term, there is an audience learning process that takes place. Low quality promotional merchandise will condition a target audience to low quality, and predictability will begin to work in the low-quality company's favor. Perceptions will no longer be mismatched. For example, if you—as a consumer—know Company X always solicits your business with a cheap phone, you may wait until the next cheap phone offer, take Company X up on it, and give the phone to your four-year-old as a birthday present. A four-year-old's perception of quality probably is more in line with what Company X can deliver.

If you are a promotional merchandise buyer for a company that can weather the negative response to cheap products until they become audience-predictable, you can make the cheap merchandise work. If you agree with this premise, it is doubtful that you as the buyer would care that the phone went to the four-year-old as long as management believed your programs were a success. Better to have gone through the hands of a four-year-old before the trash than to have gone directly into the trash.

LOGIC FAULT NUMBER THREE

The third logic fault now becomes apparent, however. Just because some very large and prestigious companies pursue a cheap-is-best promotional merchandise program doesn't mean they should be blindly followed.

An analogy that can help focus on the reasons some large corporations can get away with mismatched perceptions while other companies could be labeled as engaging in deceptive practices can be made—again with a telephone.

If a consumer calls a major corporation and the phone rings 10 times, this consumer is likely to let it ring 10 more times because he or she knows somebody is home. Prime time television ads tout the company's products and its name is a common word.

If, however, this same consumer is calling a small company, after the first set of 10 rings, the consumer is likely to assume the company is out of business or the owner is out golfing.

Build-Up for a Let-Down

Applying the same logic, a large corporation engaging in the propagation of cheap merchandise as an inducement to buy has other communications programs that can neutralize negative feelings which may arise. A national magazine that offers a dirt cheap electronic geegaw with a life span 10 minutes longer than the shipping time, can neutralize a subscriber's negative feelings with a year's worth of good reporting.

Another company that engages in the same mismatched merchandise program, may not have that same well from which to draw.

If you are a buyer who studies other promotional merchandise campaigns and wonders how companies get away with using cheap merchandise, one way to look at it is that they really are not getting away with anything. For an immediate sale, they are shifting the burden of building customer confidence and positive image to other communications avenues.

TOUGH PROBLEM, EASY ANSWER?

Sometimes merchandise buyers—invoking the Tin Man's wish—look for new and different, or bargain promotional merchandise as an easy answer to a tough problem. It can be easy to justify the purchase of this merchandise because national companies do it. As the Wizard said to the Tin Man, "As for you my galvanized friend, you want a heart. You don't know how lucky you are not to have one. Hearts will never be practical until they can be made unbreakable. Back where I come from there are men who do nothing all day but good deeds. They're called . . . good deed doers. And their hearts are no bigger than yours. But they have one thing you haven't got—a testimonial."

He gave the Tin Man a testimonial, and with it, the Tin Man realized that what he wanted he always had.

The testimonial that hopefully will show you—the corporate buyer—that you already have what you need comes from the Hard Rock Cafe—a restaurant that does more than $40 million in promotional merchandise sales a year with everyday common products. It is the intelligent application of these tested products that has allowed the Hard Rock Cafe to become a retail operation first and a restaurant second when it is viewed through its income statement.

There's not a two-billed cap or a Taiwan wiffywaffle in the product line. The merchandise is the carrier of the message, it is not the message. It reflects the tastes of the Hard Rock audience, and it serves the corporate purpose of being an advertising profit center—a concept unknown and unattainable in most corporations.

Hard Rock, Hard Facts

- Hard Rock management takes the high road with promotional merchandise. The company is not willing to risk negative reaction to its products or its image.
- The buyers for the Hard Rock Cafe do not buy new, different, or cheap products.
- The Hard Rock Cafe gives away very few giveaways.
- The company sells more than $40 million worth of promotional merchandise a year (east of the Mississippi).
- Its promotional merchandise business is larger than its restaurant business.
- The core product line is a T-shirt, sweatshirt, leather jacket, and baseball cap. There are 40 items in the line.

Environment Right

To many Americans who grew up with fast food and rock and roll, traveling to London became an exercise in avoiding local food and embracing local music. England may have been home for the world's greatest rock groups, but home cooking was not part of the travel package. Eating became a personal best test to see how much Indian food one could digest without gagging at the sight of another red chicken leg, or how many derivations of the kidney one could stomach without resorting to the next item on the bill of fare—50 or so minnows in a plastic basket, deep fried with the eyes glazed over.

American Oasis

The Hard Rock Cafe became an oasis to beef-addicted Americans. If female impersonators had been doing Sinatra imitations, Americans probably still would have packed the banquettes just to look at a menu without the word *pie* or *stew* preceded by the word *kidney.* But the founders—Isaac Tagret and Peter Morton—offered three inducements to patronize their first Hard Rock Cafe:

- American food.
- Rock music.
- Location.

The location, across the street from Buckingham Palace, was reason enough for many American rock music-loving tourists to go. Some wandered in unaware of the political implications of their actions. But many—after being turned away from venerable American family-oriented institutions like Disney World because they had long hair and back packs—seized an opportunity to thumb their nose at any establishment and fill their stomachs at the same time. The Hard Rock Cafe provided a London-based, loud, anti-establishment, nose-thumbing exercise and good American food from the moment it opened in 1972.

Promotional merchandise was a natural extension of this mind set. The want—good food, rock music, and a Hard Rock T-shirt—quickly became a need.

Food Done Well, T-Shirts Well Done

Hamburgers, french fries that weren't chips, and Cokes™ were supplemented with T-shirts about six months after the restaurant opened when Messrs. Tagret and Morton brought a few into the restaurant with the Hard Rock logo on the front. Allen Aldredge had designed a roundish graphic in three colors that proclaimed Hard Rock Cafe without a trace of subtlety.

"People were frantic to get them," says New York merchandise buyer Michael Redwine.

Perceptions had been matched. The little area in the London restaurant from which they were originally sold soon was replaced with an outdoor kiosk, "and the line for the restaurant was as long as the line for the kiosk," Mr. Redwine says.

"There is no doubt that today we're in the merchandise business," he adds. "But, the restaurant is why we're all here. People buy our T-shirts because of what we stand for: We're a rock-and-roll restaurant."

MARKET DEMOGRAPHICS ROCK SOLID

Without the aid of demographic studies, the co-owners knew their market. They were part of it. They understood the counterculture to whom they were catering, and they transformed a want into a need. The T-shirt not only carried the Hard Rock logo, but the name of the city where it was purchased. To get a Hard Rock London shirt, you had to go to London.

It is in the city name where the group dynamics really took over. Membership in the club became incrementally more exclusive, making it a more sought-after wearable than another imprinted T-shirt without a similar exclusionary modifier. The world knew the wearer walking down Chicago's Rush Street had been to London to visit not the Queen, but the Hard Rock Cafe right across the street.

Today, the New York Hard Rock Cafe keeps extra inventory in small sizes because the Japanese tourists are experiencing the same phenomenon the U.S. tourists experience in London—they need to take a shirt back home.

Hard Rock New York

One weekday night around 9 P.M. at the Manhattan Hard Rock Cafe on West 57th Street, the wait for a table is about five minutes. The line for promotional merchandise is also a five-minute queue.

While the food is very good and the waitresses, waiters, and hostess friendly and competent, it is the promotional merchandise that makes this establishment unique. The restaurant is alone in Manhattan in its pursuit of merchandise profits, save the on-again-mostly-off-again attempts at T-shirt peddling by local eateries and comedy clubs.

Hard Rock Cafe promotional merchandise is only sold in Hard Rock Cafes—"restrictive licensing," as Mr. Redwine describes it. And tonight, in New York, that means the coat room—an area so cramped revenue is measured in sales per square inch. "If you see it sold anywhere else, it's not the real thing," says Mr. Redwine.

Because of the hour, the main store—a 1,200-square-foot adjacent area with a separate entrance—is closed. To handle the evening merchandise business, the coat room is packed with the product line. A video cash register and credit card machine sit where a coat check tip bowl ought to be. A glass case hung on the wall five people in line away from the dutch door to the coat check room displays the merchandise. People already know what they want—most opt for the New York-labeled version of the T-shirt—and few bother to examine closely the other wares on display.

Mr. Redwine says 90 percent of the people who come to the Hard Rock Cafe are tourists.

A Missourian himself, Mr. Redwine says, "employees are Southern-nice or they don't last long here."

Most of the people eating or buying merchandise do look like tourists.

The merchandise moves briskly. People who come to eat also come to buy.

For those who only want to buy, there is a separate door which leads directly to the coat room. This can be a real convenience since the main entrance to the restaurant—a set of double brass doors flanked by 15 or so feet of burgundy rope threaded through chrome stanchions under the back half of a black Cadillac serving as a canopy—usually is filled with people waiting for a table.

Some patrons wear their Hard Rock clothing—purchased on previous trips. It doesn't help them get a table any sooner.

This night, the friendly doorman with a practiced British accent he wouldn't dare use in England, ushers everyone in.

"We encourage families," Mr. Redwine says. "There is no picking at the door," he says referring to the practice, honed at the city's discos, of letting only certain people into an establishment. "We treat everyone nicely, and give them a badge if they have to wait."

The badge is a Hard Rock Cafe button—a quality giveaway that makes waiting more tolerable in a city where even tourists learn waiting is a way of life.

Hard Rock, Soft Sell

Everyone participating in this event—eating or buying merchandise—has formal membership status in a casual club. Membership is free, instantly conferred when you enter and are immersed in the rock memorabilia and music. Something is going on here the way something goes on at Piazza de Popolo in Rome on a Sunday late in the afternoon. Diverse personalities are together because of a common interest, and the more memories these groups take, whether in the shape of a sweatshirt or a good time, the more advertising they give the Hard Rock Cafe. It is a very fair trade—the empirical example of the power of word-of-mouth (word-of-chest in the case of a T-shirt) advertising from satisfied customers.

The same tableau is played out at the other Hard Rock Cafes around the world every day.

Making It Happen

What the customers don't see, however, is how the merchandise finds its way to the cluttered cloak room.

Getting there, in this case, isn't always half the fun. Mr. Redwine is responsible for purchasing the approximately $11 million a year worth of merchandise for the New York operation.

"We take bets on what will go wrong. We know something will go wrong with every order," he says, grinning.

"No matter how carefully you prepare the purchase order, no matter how many pre-production samples you get, no matter how completely you think the manufacturer understands what you want, something will go wrong." Mr. Redwine adds, "Don't even ask me to order something new, untested, or from an unknown supplier. I don't need the headache.

"We are fanatic, picky. The colors have to be right, the embroidery perfect, the size and the color have to be exactly what we want. We use only 100 percent cotton Hanes™ Beefy T or equivalent T-shirts, only the best caps and jackets," Mr. Redwine explains.

A glimpse into the purchasing habits of the promotional merchandise buyer whose purchases rival many department stores' shows several interesting points that can be applicable to promotional merchandise buyers at all levels—a chance to profit from the Hard Rock's hard knocks.

Although the Hard Rock generally knows its suppliers' profit margins, Mr. Redwine does not think it is critical that a corporate buyer know the profit structure in small deals.

Profit from Us

"We expect our suppliers to make a profit. In one case I told the supplier to increase his profit. If they don't make a profit, they won't be around next year to serve us. This means I have to find a new supplier," Mr. Redwine explains.

"The backbone of our purchasing is to get the best possible quality for the least possible price. We expect our customers feel the same way, whether they're buying our T-shirt or a burger. With quality versus cost, quality always wins.

"For our T-shirts we work directly with Hanes distributors or our own private label mills in the United States. All our T-shirts are produced in America. I know the cost for the blank shirt, how much it costs to print it, pack it, ship it, and I know the mark-ups. We inspect all merchandise, and deduct from invoices all unacceptable goods. We do not return goods."

Mr. Redwine explains that since the Hard Rock logo so often appears on counterfeit merchandise, to return defective merchandise to suppliers is to invite them to re-sell the goods to small street retailers: "My fear is that when the merchandise is returned to the front door of the vendor, it will go out the back door to the odd lot buyer."

Merchandise Donated to Charity

"Our purchase orders clearly state that if the merchandise is unacceptable, we will not pay for it. We will donate it to a charity, however. If the merchandise is flawed slightly, we notify the supplier, renegotiate the price and sell it at a discount at our stores."

Perfect Hard Rock T-shirts sell in New York for $11. "We think this is the price point and quality level our customers want. We could go to a more expensive T-shirt like the Champion [brand], but we would have to sell it for $14, and we think this is more than our customers want to pay for a T-shirt."

This same philosophy extends throughout the 40-item product line, which includes T-shirts and sweatshirts in white, black, and one other color depending on the season; baseball caps in white and black with embroidered logos on the front; denim jackets from Levi Strauss; wool and leather college awards jackets; an all-leather jacket; a polo-style shirt; Ray Ban sunglasses; metal Cadillac shaped key tags; lapel pins in the shape of a guitar and the Hard Rock logo; a teddy bear; a binder; and Swatch-type watches.

"We try to make a connection with every member of the family and a connection with rock-and-roll through our merchandise.

"We also know our T-shirt may not always be as popular as it is today, so we are working on new ways to use products that will achieve our objectives," Mr. Redwine says.

One of these ways is the Hard Rock Cafe's association with charitable causes, which it promotes through merchandise.

Program at Home with Homeless

A co-op program with Coca-Cola to benefit the homeless was publicized with a special edition Hard Rock-Coke™ T-shirt advertised on Coke™ cans. Television and radio performances—

live from Hard Rock—with complementing merchandise, further keep the name in front of target audiences.

The key here is that rather than take a chance on an unknown product, the Hard Rock Cafe has preferred to find new ways to use proven merchandise.

"Even so," Mr. Redwine says, "we expect problems. If I know a supplier, I know I won't generally have trouble with the merchandise. Maybe with shipping, though. Ninety percent of the time the problem comes from a really stupid human error.

"If I have to babysit with suppliers, it means dropping them, and I hate to drop a supplier because it means I have to start all over again with a new one."

Laundry List for Clean Deals

Although Mr. Redwine says he continually reviews suppliers while he is working with them, there also is a formal monthly review that documents problems.

"We always have three suppliers for each product so that we are not put in a bind if we have to drop a supplier."

Mr. Redwine recommends calling three suppliers with your purchasing specs before buying. "Know what your needs are. Be ready to discuss your budget, timing, type of print, quality of product and shipping details.

"Ask for a production sample," he says, although he admits that if your order is small, suppliers may not want to go to the trouble, or you may not want to pay them for it.

"Be very clear about who will pay for extra costs including screens, packing, shipping, damage, loss, and rush charges."

About rush charges, he says, "buy as far out as possible. We purchase six months out with a 30- to 60-day delivery window. Never pay more than 50 percent up front, and try to avoid up front payments as much as possible. Sometimes they are unavoidable, but usually they can be negotiated.

"Keep your art simple, provide accurate drawings and identify all PMS colors. If you don't have a PMS book, buy one at an art store. Tell the supplier exactly where you want your art to appear on the product.

"Compare the responses to your conversations with suppliers covering these points as well as the price, and choose a supplier based on your priorities. We never choose on price alone," he says.

"And then wait for the problems."

CHAPTER 5

GIZMO CHAOS: WHEN EVERYTHING GOES WRONG

The premise of this chapter is that you, the buyer, want quality merchandise—whether you are buying a 10-cent balloon or a $200 clock; that you want this merchandise manufactured to your specifications; and that you want to learn what you can do to ensure that you get what you want.

What is gizmo chaos?

- In the privacy of Air Force One, President Reagan gives American flags to the press to commemorate the administration's first U.S.-U.S.S.R. summit. The flags have 48 stars
- Peninsula Medical Center gives out magnets in the shape and color of adhesive strip bandages that say "Call Us When It Hurts." There is no phone number on the magnets.
- The A.T. Cross Company takes more than six months to produce 110 pens. The logo is wrong, and it takes three more months to make the correction.

Virtually every merchandise order is an exercise in controlling or surrendering to chaos. Sometimes the buyers are spectators to the chaos; most of the time the agent and the manufacturer view this chaos, and the buyer sees the result.

Everybody—agents, manufacturers, and buyers—can take equal credit for promulgating the chaos. It is born of general sloppiness, cost-cutting, outright deception, and incompetence. Ad specialty manufacturing generally is not a gentlemen's marketplace, but rather a worldwide, undisciplined, cents-off sale where most often pride and craftsmanship are subjugated to price and carelessness. The Swiss Army knife manufacturers have been one of the exceptions, but even here, one of the two manufacturers—Victorinox—no longer offers the touted lifetime guarantee. Wenger, the smaller of the two official suppliers of knives to the Swiss Army, still warrantees its knives forever.

INDIRECT CONTROL

Although you, as a buyer, can be an equal partner in chaos, you are the only person who can ultimately control it because you have the power to give or take away business. Your control, however, is indirect because you cannot stand on the factory floor and make sure the imprint on your geegaw is sharp and straight each time the hot stamping machine comes down on it. And, when you're Larry Speaks and you're 30,000 feet over the Atlantic Ocean on your way to Red Square giving out the American Flag commemorative gifts, it's too late to exercise control when the media people start counting the stars.

Exercising your control takes time and timing, money, experience, and the ability to recognize exceptional as well as unexceptional suppliers. If you are not willing to devote measured amounts of time, money, brains, and experience, you will receive a measured dose of mediocrity—or worse—from your suppliers.

To help explain the boundaries of your indirect control, a short story: My sister and brother-in-law have (at the time I'm writing this) an 18-month-old daughter. Father Mark takes her for walks in Central Park a few blocks away from their New York City apartment. He describes his experiences walking through the park with daughter Tosha as being similar to walking a basset hound. She stops to handle, eat, and play with everything she sees as she meanders through the park, unaware of time and space. Working with manufacturers is like taking Tosha—or a basset hound—for a walk. You may have the ultimate control, but Tosha, the basset hound, and the manufacturer are going to do pretty much what they want until you interject your own structure. How and when you shorten the leash on a manufacturer will determine how and when you get your merchandise.

SPEAK CLEARLY

The starting point is the first time you talk with the manufacturer or its authorized agent. If you clearly establish early in your relationship what you demand—quality, price, delivery, etc.—you stand a much better chance of getting it. Begin with an unequivocal statement that you will not accept or pay for merchandise that does not meet a minimum standard you set. Period. Be very clear. Do this before you start fingering the samples or browsing through the catalogs. Also explain that any unaccepted merchandise cannot be dumped on the odd-lot market, used as samples, or as items in catalogs. Your unacceptable merchandise must be destroyed. (This will protect your trademarked logo from appearing on shoddy merchandise which will be sold at flea markets and city street corners.)

Explain too, that you are not interested in negotiating a lower price once any substandard merchandise reaches your office. (Many manufacturers and their agents will offer to sell the merchandise at a reduced rate—what they would get on the odd-lot market—and many buyers see this as a bargain. Even if you are one of these buyers, now is not the time to discuss your predilection for damaged goods.)

DREAM AT YOUR OWN RISK

When buying merchandise, you usually get what you don't think you're asking for. A vivid example of what you say not being what the supplier hears comes from a scene in the movie *Mr. Blandings Builds His Dream House.* Mr. Blandings (Cary Grant) is showing the painter—who is sloppily dressed, inattentive, arrogant—through each unfinished room in his new home describing in minute detail the exact colors he wants for each room. "Blue" is not an apt description of the color of the living room. It is described as "robin's egg blue with a hint of a summer sky" or some such descriptive prose. After a three-minute monologue when the two—Mr. Blandings and the painter—have toured four rooms, the painter reviews the color choices: "Red, Yellow, Blue and Green. Got it," he says as Mr. Blandings watches his dream house turn into the nightmare in Westport, Connecticut.

The situation in the movie could have been avoided with a simple color chart. Mr. Blandings could have chosen the exact shades he wanted, the painter would have mixed the colors, and all would have been peaceful. But it didn't happen that way. The level of detail for even the most simple paint—or promotional merchandise—order is boggling. Most buyers' eyes glaze over when confronted with these decisions, but their eyes bug out when what they thought the manufacturer understood was their order is really a reflection of what he had in stock.

TIME & TIMING ON HILTON HEAD

Even when you are specific, the chances of an order getting turned upside down are great, and if you have not planned ahead, you will be forced to take the merchandise you do not want. This is where the second How To Reduce Gizmo Chaos theorem comes in: Give yourself time, and be cognizant of your timing.

Example:

PMS 185 is a trade designation for red ink. PMS 285 is blue. When *The Island Packet,* a newspaper on Hilton Head Island, ordered 500 red 16-ounce plastic cups (PMS 185), they got 500 in blue. Simple mistake. Somebody confused the two ink identification numbers. Unfortunately publisher Ben Banks didn't say when he placed his order, "I'll take red, unless they come out blue."

To the contrary, the color was set in a blazing sun—a combination of reds, oranges, and yellows.

The slogan, "Get Up with the Packet," told the island of 10,000 that the newspaper was becoming a daily morning paper.

The Island Packet management made the decision in 1985 to move from a three-times a week afternoon paper to a daily morning paper and decided to commemorate the event with an island party—a black-tie affair held at an island hotel complete with cocktails, dinner, and a revue performed by the local theater group. Promotional merchandise was to play an important role.

In addition to the plastic cups, white canvas tote bags with the three-color logo were ordered, and in them would go the first morning edition of the paper, a three-color button with similar graphics, promotional literature, and an event program.

The 16-ounce imprinted red cups would replace the hotel's usual 12-ounce models to further state the theme and keep the lines short at the portable bars during the cocktail hour.

Blue Sun Blues

The cups with the blue sunburst arrived first—a day before the event. It was decided to use them anyway, since there was no time to re-do the order. The tote bags were due the morning of the event. That morning came and went. The manufacturer swore the bags were shipped overnight. UPS had lost the shipment. The bags were found in Beaufort, South Carolina after an hour of screaming at the nameless voices in "The Tightest Ship in the Shipping Business." *The Packet* sent its own representatives to pick them up because the "Tight Ship" couldn't deliver them until the next day—after the event.

Laying Blame

So far, everyone is to blame for this chaos. The newspaper should have ordered the merchandise earlier. The cup manufacturer should have followed instructions on the purchase order. UPS should have delivered the tote bags on time, and at least, should have made an extra effort to deliver them once they were found in another city. In everyone's defense: UPS can't stop its entire operation to locate and deliver one package, and The Island

Packet assumed the manufacturer could get the order right with a short lead time.

Now, back to the story.

Hilton Head is a small island. It took little time for the chaos story to spread, and it became a topic at the formal dinner. Most guests laughed at the blue cups, and those who had bought promotional merchandise before understood too well the symptoms of chaos. These veterans offered their own versions of the chaos they had endured.

Advanced Chaos

What was happening now was advanced chaos. It was no longer just an internal logistical problem, the chaos had a life of its own and was news—like when the media started counting the stars aboard Air Force One.

Aside from the obvious distasteful feeling of being in the vortex of gizmo chaos as the buyer or the agent, its negative power now extended to the target audience. It is at this point at which careers are stopped cold. It was not the message *The Island Packet* cared to impart—the one about the blue sun or the lost and found adventure with the tote bags. The chaos, as its name implies, superceded *The Packet's* message.

To his credit, publisher Banks is a man not easily flustered. Being in the newspaper business, he is comfortable in an environment where his control of events is tenuous at best. He fielded the barbs well and deftly changed the subject every chance he got. After all, in a world where radio station disc jockeys interrupt music to tell you their station plays continuous music, what's so chaotic about a blue sun?

NO CREDIBILITY

The trials of the Hilton Head newspaper notwithstanding, the single biggest contributor to promotional merchandise chaos is when everyone—buyer, agent, and manufacturer—underrate its importance and overuse the medium. Promotional merchandise is often the last topic considered when the brains of an organization sit down to discuss the new building, the company picnic, the sales contest, the quality improvement program, the retirement dinner, or the sports league—for good reason, too. Dealing in this arena is often distasteful and usually confusing and irritating. A lot of cheesy characters with stained ties are apt to darken the corporate portals peddling all manner of imprintable items and asking for money up front. People you wouldn't talk to at a downtown bus station will be phoning trying to convince you to buy their particular geegaw for your next event.

TIME & TIMING AGAIN

It is not extraordinary that buyers put off this particular torture until the last possible day. But to put it off is to invite chaos. Better to find the agent who more closely resembles your corporate culture than to continue dealing with characters at the eleventh hour.

Sometimes, however, your agent and you are helpless. Time and timing are the only effective countermeasures to employ against chaos, as the following vignettes illustrate.

Blue Cheeks Make Dad See Red

Bill Artman, a project engineer at ASEA Brown Boveri, a Swiss heavy machinery company, ordered T-shirts. It was a simple straightforward order—navy blue imprint on the front. They arrived a few days late, but a false deadline to the manufacturer allowed for this late delivery.

Bill gave away the first shirts the day they arrived. It was Friday. An employee picked one up and took it home. Saturday he wore it. As the day wore on, the found his way to the couch and fell asleep. His two-year-old daughter found her way to the couch and fell asleep on his chest, her face on his new white T-shirt with the navy blue imprint. An hour or so later, he woke up. He glanced down at his daughter and saw blue where rosy cheeks used to be. He was not amused at the fact that, as he learned later, the T-shirt screener did not allow the ink to dry properly so it came off on his sleeping daughter's face.

About the same time he and his daughter were experiencing the T-shirt blues, another employee who had taken a shirt home had finished working in the yard and threw his new T-shirt into the washer along with other dirty clothes. The clothes came out clean—and blue—when the T-shirt ink ran during the wash.

This was totally a manufacturing problem—carelesssness on the part of the people screening the T-shirts. The manufacturer took back the shirts, but if they were needed for a specific event, or given to the public, ASEA Brown Boveri could have had legal as well as image problems. Mr. Artman solved the problem by using another manufacturer because he had the luxury of time. Time was what averted advanced chaos.

Ribbons of Chaos

Timing, too, can either work for or against you when you are buying promotional merchandise.

Take the case of the opening of a major resort hotel. The grand opening called for gifts wrapped in color coordinated boxes with fancy ribbon. Except, the agent in charge of getting the ribbon didn't realize that this largely Jewish, New York-based industry wouldn't be in any mood to supply a small order the day before Passover. Timing. A New York agent got the ribbon at almost three times the normal price. A more common example of bad timing is ordering calendars in November.

The point here is that to avoid chaos, you must be cognizant of both industry customs and national and regional religious and civic holidays. Many suppliers close during July. The Advertising Specialty Institute (ASI), a trade group, publishes lists of manufacturers' vacation and holiday closings, as well as cut-off dates for Christmas orders. The latest 1988 list shows cut-off Christmas dates of 981 suppliers around the country. Agents have access to these lists, and they should consult the lists whenever an order is likely to be stopped cold by a holiday.

In an accompanying ASI survey, suppliers gave the following reasons for ordering Christmas merchandise early:

- Price is locked in. No rush charges.
- Items are in stock.

- Overnight delivery services are not needed.
- Corrections can be made when errors occur.

ASI management said in its note to agents, "It's all painfully obvious," describing the survey results, "but it bears repeating simply because it is so often ignored."

The second, but no less obvious point, here is that if you buy during the off season—a calendar order in February—you will not only have time on your side, but price discounts as well. (If your calendar supplier will not give you a substantial discount for ordering before April, find another supplier.)

FOUR-WEEK DELIVERY

In the promotional merchandise business, four weeks is not this time next month. To illustrate this point, picture yourself ordering 1,000 pens. The catalog says production time is four weeks. The date is November 7, 1988. When will you get your pens, if there are no screw-ups?

a. December 5, four weeks from November 7.
b. January 23, 1989, 11 weeks after you place the order.

The answer is b. Here's why:

November 7: You place the order, give the agent your logo and the additional copy you want on the pens.

November 8: Election day. Agent does not work.

November 9: Agent takes art and copy to layout house where type is set, art reduced for position and mechanical is produced.

November 10: Late afternoon, mechanical is ready.

November 11: Veterans Day. Nobody works.

November 12 and 13: Weekend.

November 14: Agent mails purchase order and mechanical to supplier.

November 17: Supplier receives order.

November 18: Supplier enters order into computer.

November 19 and 20: Weekend.

November 21: Day 1 of production begins.

Here is where the four-week (28 working days) production schedule begins—two full weeks from the time you placed your order. You may be expecting your pens two weeks from today, but if you are, you will be disappointed.

November 22: Day 2 of production.

November 23: Half-day. Everyone leaves early for Thanksgiving.

November 24: Thanksgiving. Nobody works.

November 26 and 27: Weekend.

November 28: Day 3 of production. (Remember, we need 28 days of production to get the order out, and Santa's coming.)

November 29–30: Production days 4 and 5.

December 1: Production day 6.

December 2: Friday before Hanukkah, half-day.

December 3 and 4: Weekend.

December 5: Day after Hanukkah, many workers take off.

December 6–9: Production days 7, 8, 9, and 10.

December 10 and 11: Weekend.

Halfway Home

December 12–16: Production days 11, 12, 13, 14, and 15. (Production is halfway through.)

December 17 and 18: Weekend.

December 19–23: Production days 16, 17, 18, 19, and 20. (We are lucky in 1988 because Christmas Eve is on Saturday and Christmas Day is on Sunday. The production schedule won't be further disrupted by this holiday.)

December 24 and 25: Weekend.

December 26–30: Large percentage of workers take vacation days. Many suppliers are closed for some or all of these days.

Happy New Year

December 31 and January 1: Weekend.

January 2: Day after New Year's. Nobody works.

January 3–6: Production days 21, 22, 23 and 24.

January 7 and 8: Weekend.

January 9–12: Production days 25, 26, 27, and 28. At this point, your pens are shipped. Most likely they will be shipped UPS ground. UPS guarantees seven-day delivery anywhere in the continental United States–seven working days, of course.

January 13: Shipping day 1.

January 14 and 15: Weekend.

January 16–20: Shipping days 2, 3, 4, 5, and 6.

January 21 and 22: Weekend.

January 23: Shipping day 7. Your pens should arrive.

Remember the Pens We Ordered?

Seventy-eight calendar days after you placed your order—11 weeks later—your merchandise arrives.

This is not the longest "four-week" production schedule of the year. Most suppliers close for at least two weeks during the summer: there are the president's days in February, Memorial Day, Labor Day, Fourth of July weekends, Rosh Hashanah, Yom Kippur, and Easter. There is shipping time to consider, which can take two or three weeks for large orders that go by truck; there is art preparation time; and preproduction sample approval time.

Send Me a One-Off

Preproduction samples are the biggest obstacle to production schedules after holidays. When the one-off is done, the job is taken off the production line while the sample is sent to you. It can take five working days to reach your office. You might take two or more days to show it to the right people and approve it. You can phone your approval, which means the job can be immediately rescheduled for production. This assumes, however, that the preproduction sample is correctly manufactured—most are not. When there are changes, you may have to send the sample back and use up another seven days' time in shipping. Preproduction samples can easily add 15–20 calendar days to the production period.

August 1, Class Rings Arrive

You are inviting chaos if you don't learn to read the promotional merchandise calendar, and are instead lulled into thinking four weeks is this time next month, or 15 days is two weeks from now. Many high school advisors have made the mistake of not knowing how to read the promotional merchandise calendar, and the yearbooks and class rings arrived "on time" in the middle of the summer.

You might assume that as a smart buyer who is not necessarily interested in learning how to read a new calendar, you could simply give the "must have" date to the agent or supplier and expect it to be met.

Most of the time these conversations go something like this:

BUYER TO AGENT:

I need it Friday, the 18th, can you get it?

AGENT:

I'll try. If I can't, will you accept a five-legged armadillo at 50 percent more instead of a four-legged one?

BUYER:

Only if I have to. Let me know.

Now the agent is participating in buyer-originated chaos. He or she begins to look for merchandise that can be produced by the 18th. Whether it will communicate the right message to the right audience is of little importance now. This, more than any other reason, is why so many companies give away pens and buttons at trade shows. They can be produced quickly. It is also the reason most balloons lose their logos when they are inflated.

IMAGE & LOGO DISAPPEAR

Whenever an event is planned, someone decides—usually too late—that balloons would add to the festive atmosphere, so a couple hundred are ordered with the company logo. When the balloons arrive in their little box (a lot of deflated balloons will fit in a small box), the logo looks sharp and dense; but add a little helium, and like magic the logo fades. Buyers accept these poor quality imprints most often because of time and price. Manufacturing processes that produce clean sharp logos on inflated balloons are available. But these balloons can't be had overnight like the fade-away specials.

What good is a logo that only looks good when the balloon is deflated? If you were in a classroom and someone asked that question, most people would answer that the logo is of no good use and probably is detrimental to the corporate image. This substandard imprinting process—textbook communication chaos—has survived for the same reason that the longer a person stays at a singles bar, the more likely it is that he or she will find a soulmate. As the hour grows later, the remainders at the bar tend to look better. Two days before the maternity party for the vice president, a faded logo on a cheap balloon looks pretty good to some buyers.

FADE-AWAY SPECIALS

In more sober moments, one could reflect on the fact that a corporation will pay hundreds of thousands of dollars to have a corporate identity program created, pay an equal amount on stationery and signage to display this logo, and pay enough to keep a cadre of art directors busy making sure all advertisements conform to strict corporate standards. In one chaotic moment, however, the fade-away specials surface. Often, even when there is time to produce the better balloon imprints, the seemingly rational buyer will opt for fading logo because of cost differences (pennies per balloon), proving that he or she is penny-wise and image-foolish. If you accept the low quality imprint, you are the classic example of the buyer who underrates promotional merchandise, and then overworks it. You don't care what they look like, but you expect people who see them to be impressed. If your attitude is "They're going to burst anyway," buy unimprinted balloons at the party or stationery store on your way to work. They won't have the negative effect of poorly displaying your company logo, and they will keep you a step ahead of chaos.

CAN'TS & DON'TS

Staying a step ahead may be all you can do in the promotional merchandise business, but it may be enough. If you are serious about eliminating the chaos, there are several things you *can't* do:

- Have a brainstorm on your way to work one morning resulting in the perfect merchandise for the sales meeting scheduled for the day after tomorrow. Chances are you've been planning the sales meeting for six months. Gizmos without chaos deserve more than a day and a half.
- Delegate the purchase of promotional merchandise to the lowest person on your team, make yourself unavailable for consultation, reserve your right to veto anything, impose strict budgets, and then whine about the chaos.
- Call five promotional merchandise agents and five suppliers you pick randomly from the Yellow Pages, make them jump through your corporate hoops, then beat them down on price and choose one.
- Give your supplier only enough information to be dangerous, such as: "We need something for the sales conference." Don't tell him or her what you've used in the past, what management

hates, what management likes, or anything else that will help the supplier meet your needs. Picture a stranger walking up to you and saying, "Tomorrow is my brother's birthday, what should I get him?" and pose an equally unanswerable question to your supplier.

• Don't bother to work with your supplier. Don't ask for preproduction samples, don't proof screens or dies, and don't answer questions that come up. Let the problems resolve themselves. (In the early 1980s, Minolta ordered Random House dictionaries and thesauruses that had the following copy screened on the front cover: "For the meaning of 'dependability' see P. 244. Or see your Minolta dealer." The books were directed at secretaries who were thought to be copier buying influences. The problem was that the first group of books had the wrong page number. When the hapless participant turned to the page originally suggested on the cover, there was no definition of "dependability." There were not any words that even began with the letter "D." Chaos ensued. Random House reprinted the covers, but promotion schedules had to be revised, time was lost, and advanced chaos set in.)

WHAT'S YOUR RENT?

Before you can take steps to eliminate chaos, you have to decide whether you recognize promotional merchandise as a legitimate and powerful method of communicating a message. If you don't, you are relegated to forever buying balloons with fading logos. If you do see them as a powerful medium, ask yourself another question. How much is your mortgage (or rent) payment? If it is less than $850 (1988 dollars) a month, merchandise without chaos will seem exorbitantly expensive to you, and you will be forever bargain hunting and inviting chaos. If your rent or mortgage payment is more than $850 a month, you probably have a better overall understanding of what things cost in this world, and you will be able to come to terms with the actual costs of promotional merchandise—in dollars and time—sans chaos.

TROPHY SHRAPNEL

This last example of gizmo chaos must be disguised heavily. Serious career moves downward have already taken place since the great trophy shrapnel scandal, and discussing it is worse than rubbing salt in corporate wounds.

However, it needs to be told because it is a graphic example of what not to do.

The story begins innocently enough with a meeting arranged by an agent with suppliers and the buyer. The product being discussed—we'll call it a trophy—was for the best, the greatest, the most wonderful job done in the entire company. Money, at this meeting, was no object. "Beauty," "art," "status," "great design"—these were the words bandied about during this heady meeting where a nervous secretary poured coffee and served danish on a very expensive imported wood conference table.

The meeting ended with the agreement that the supplier would get back to the buyer with prices for a preproduction sample. There was, of course, just enough time to get the sample done, approved and the final trophy completed before the black tie affair at an exclusive resort would be held to award it.

Stop Right There

Sometime during the night after the first meeting, the corporate buyer got cold feet. He or she (a further disguise) decided to save money and have a cheap version made using the same basic design. The flaw in this thinking was that a cheap version of the design wouldn't have the same tolerances as the expensive version. The trophy, having five different parts, would not—in the cheap version—have these parts securely fastened to each other.

The evening came. The trophy sat beside the dias waiting for the moment of presentation. The speeches were winding down. People were burping their last burps after the very expensive and rich dinner. The chairman reached over to pick up the trophy, and with all the force of a Midwest-born athlete cum chairman, he grabbed it by the base. Trophy shrapnel, in the form of the four remaining pieces flew towards the audience with the same force applied to the base to bring it close to him. Vice presidents dove to retrieve the projectiles before they hit the floor. Everyone tittered as their eyes fixed on the buyer. Nobody could come up with a line that would relieve the tension. Not until later did some of the more astute in the audience realize that the entire episode had been captured on video tape, and that tape now commands a high price within the company.

Nobody ever asked how much the trophy cost, or thanked the buyer for saving the company money.

CHAPTER 6

HOW EFFECTIVE IS IT? EVALUATING YOUR PROGRAM

Eighty-six percent of respondents said yes. They would use the firm that gave them a geegaw or a doodad.

The question was: There are two vendors, both having the same product and prices. One uses these items. The other does not. You have dealt with neither before. Which one would you be more favorably disposed towards buying from?

Eighty-six percent said they would buy from the company that gave them an ad specialty. The main reason: "Their name is familiar to me," and, "they gave me something extra," respondents said.

Sixty-one percent of the respondents had received ad specialties in the past, and ninety-nine percent said they enjoyed receiving them. Ninety percent said they felt favorable towards the company that gave them the ad specialties. Ninety-three percent said they felt this type of promotion is effective. A composite of responses showed that specialty advertising improves name recall and is a subtle reminder.

These findings are part of a very small universe of research on specialty advertising's effectiveness. Even so, the results are dramatic when compared with responses to equivalent questions about television, radio, or print advertising.

FOR NOBODY'S EYES ONLY

Advertising specialties and premiums generally have escaped the researchers' and pollsters' eyes, and nobody will admit to knowing absolutely whether it is more effective to print your message on baseball caps or to buy television time during baseball games. It's anybody's educated guess, and because it's virtually impossible to compare ad specialties to other advertising mediums, the word *guess* can be interpreted literally.

Addressing this particular ad specialty versus television question, Fred Danzig—editor of Advertising Age—offers his own question: "Can Bill Cosby or the Superbowl do in 30 seconds what a year's worth of T-shirts could do if you only spent half as much on the T-shirts? I don't know."

He rephrases the question and makes it a statement: "I would hate to be the account supervisor who says 'cancel Monday night football and buy ashtrays for every bar in America with the client's logo on them.'

"Maybe it's easier with the Olympics or the Superbowl to recommend ad specialties, but in between, it's hard to get an ad agency—under pressure to get the revenue stream up—to recommend something that may come out of the media budget and go to another company."

THE MEDIA ISN'T AD SPECIALTIES

Mr. Danzig's sentiments reflect several realities of advertising agencies' perceptions of advertising specialties.

"Agencies are keyed to media programs," he says. "People on accounts are concerned about traditional programs they have inherited. They don't stop to listen to the guy knocking on the door with a new doodad. They are not sure of his track record, if it is made in Hong Kong, if it is available in sufficient quantities. They prefer to wear blinders and not get caught up in that kind of deal. The [ad specialty] industry has a huge selling job to do before they [ad specialties] are integrated into programs."

How restrictive these blinders are and how big the selling job is becomes clear in the following comment from David Ogilvy: "I know nothing about your subject . . . ," was his response to why promotional merchandise was often ignored by ad agencies. Mr. Ogilvy, founder of Ogilvy & Mather Advertising, pioneer of advertising communication techniques throughout the 1950s and 60s, is the person responsible for creating the Hathaway-shirt man who wears—interestingly—a blinder of sorts over one eye.

SHORT-TERM

Promotional merchandise is viewed at many agencies—when it is viewed at all—as part of short-term promotions; and today, Mr. Danzig says, "many agencies are focusing attention on long-term ways of meeting competition—measures to elevate the product, brand, or service above the commodity level. Foreign products have tended to turn everything into a commodity—everything is price sensitive. Advertising is trying to add value to the product, and agencies may be saying that [promotional] merchandise doesn't add to this objective.

"A few years ago sales promotions were becoming more popular," he says. "Ad agencies beat them back. Now sales promotion people say their programs should mesh with an ad program.

"Ad agencies have expended a lot of money saying it all comes down to creative, not ad specialties or sales promotions," he says.

SAATCHI'S PETISI CONCURS

Robert J. Petisi, president and CEO of Saatchi Saatchi Promotions in New York, has similar feelings about the role of ad specialties and premiums. His theory of why they do not enjoy the same level of use as other forms of advertising is "that as far back as the 1950s Madison Avenue rejected the sales promotion discipline because it drained profits. The more polite euphemism for not using it was that promotional merchandise—in the eyes of the sophisticated advertising executive—was suspect as a true marketing tactic.

"Madison Avenue undermined this option—a more targeted way to get to the consumer—in favor of broad-based advertising mediums. Advertising executives ignored target market segmentation across the board, and this happened to include promotions and promotional merchandise including point of sale. Today we are trying to strike a balance between brand image awareness and promotions which can deal with point of sale."

KID-PACK PROMOTIONS

Mr. Petisi's job is to recognize the power of promotional merchandise and promotions, and use it to his client's benefit. He uses as an example the fast food industry's meals directed specifically to children: "They typically are more expensive than if the same foods were bought separately, but they are packaged in a fancy container and usually include some kind of promotional merchandise. And," he adds, "they bring the kids and the parents into the restaurant."

Returning to the historical view, Mr. Petisi recounts the days of the Alka Seltzer and Volkswagen commercials that reached out to willing consumers with a product solution to a need in the marketplace: "There was no need for target market segmentation with products like these in this environment. Everybody watched television in the evening. There were no VCR's, people weren't as mobile, there was no cable, no health craze, home computers or health food. People were in front of the televisions from 7 to 10 P.M. and they could be reached with brand advertising. Today," he says, "the world is one of target market segmentation, and this is where promotional merchandise excels."

He mentions the cosmetic industry, which Saatchi serves, and discusses the "all image, all style" target marketing that includes a gift with purchase aimed at the higher level buyer of products like Aramis. Here the premium is tied directly to the quality of the buyer.

He goes on to say that corporate recognition of programs like these is growing at a very fast rate among his clients: "Premiums are becoming more and more sophisticated. They are adding value to the product and supporting brand image. They have a wide appeal; they tie into current events like movies and television shows. It is a very solid business."

TOUGH TO MEASURE

Still, he admits it's tough to measure their effectiveness against other forms of media or against alternate choices of merchandise.

Ad specialties have their own power and allure that has not been sufficiently quantified. Even if advertising agencies or corporate managers wanted to substitute ad specialties for conventional media buys, the data to justify this decision is so scant that it has to make gut sense to all parties involved. If it doesn't, it can't be argued with numbers.

Mr. Petisi gives examples of trade promotions done for Hertz whose market was 100,000 travel agents, and while they are an admitted success—business increased—it was Mr. Petisi's and his client's feel for what merchandise would work that was the determining factor in product purchases, not reams of data.

Few agencies, unless they have a specialist at hand such as Mr. Petisi, are willing to make this leap into merchandise. They will all admit that ad specialties and premiums have a place, but often they know where that place isn't, rather than where it is, and "it isn't in my budget unless it can be empirically justified," say many media buyers.

DOODADS ARE GIFT PROMOTIONS

The 80 people who were interviewed for the survey noted at the beginning of this chapter don't begin to constitute an empirical justification for using ad specialties. Many people don't even know what to call them, let alone how to measure their effectiveness. (In the 80-person survey, 30 percent of respondents—the highest percentage—called them "gift promotions.") Additionally, they are much more complicated than conventional advertising because they ask the audience to participate in the message.

Mr. Danzig describes them as, "asking me to make room for them in my life. I have to decide how to use them myself or whether to give them to somebody. They stop the mental traffic while you deal with them. Television and print advertising doesn't do this."

RESEARCH EMERGING

In ad specialty marketing and research circles, one professor—James Gould—is emerging as a leader. With him, the teaching and doing adage proclaiming who can do and who must teach, does not have merit. Professor Gould can do and does teach, and doing comes in the form of working with a local ad specialty firm. Teaching takes place on the fifth floor of a modern mid-rise building in White Plains, New York at Pace University's Lubin Graduate School of Business.

By his own admission he is a better professor than a peddler, but he is both nonetheless, and he is as demonstrably proud of his selling efforts as he is thankful for the indulgence of the local ad specialty firm—N. Donald Edwards, Inc. in Stamford, Connecticut. His war stories about trinkets and geegaws, trade shows, and customers are as practical as they are scholarly.

PAPER TRAINED

With more than 20 research papers devoted to ad specialties (he is responsible for the 80-person survey quoted earlier), what may seem like his seat-of-the-pants decision to a prospective customer is actually information from the unofficial seat of knowledge and professorial thought on ad specialties and premiums. He is ahead of his time, slowly creating a power base where no power and no base existed when he began his work five or so years ago.

Professor Gould is alternately embraced and rejected by the geegaw and trinket establishment, and he is the kind of scholar who gives the impression of preferring to be embraced.

"When I first started studying 'promotional incentive items' and the entire 'promotional incentive media' (terms he has coined), I tried to join SAAGNY [a local ad specialty trade organization in the northeast—Specialty Advertising Association of Greater New York], but they wouldn't have me because I wasn't selling or producing ad specialties."

Unlike the local group, the national ad specialty organizations welcomed Professor Gould, and while they may not agree with all his findings, his admission to the organizations was based on his scholarship not salesmanship. It is these organizations' publications that first entertained Professor Gould's thoughts on the industry. He took courses given by the Specialty Advertising Association International and received a CAS (Certified Advertising Specialty) degree.

THE BIG QUESTIONS

Professor Gould's studies tend to focus on what he, Mr. Danzig, and Mr. Petisi would agree are the two most basic but still unanswered questions in the industry:

- How do you measure the effectiveness, or lack thereof, of a promotional merchandise program? (*The $3 Billion Question* as one of his papers on the subject calls it referring to the size of the ad specialty industry when the study was done in 1987.)
- How can buyers buy what recipients want? "Preferences from a recipient's perspective," in his terms.

The pursuit of answers to these questions has taken him out in the field, into buyers' offices, and to the people who have received somebody's promotional merchandise. His published work—while admirable within the confines of the promotional merchandise industry—is inconclusive and dwarfed by even casual efforts of agencies and national research firms that determine the effectiveness of traditional advertising media.

But Professor Gould is undaunted.

REESE'S CUP SEMINAR

While professor James Gould, editor Fred Danzig, and sales promotion executive Robert Petisi have never met and were interviewed separately, their pursuits—when combined—are like the promotional merchandise equivalent of getting "peanut butter in my chocolate." While this Reese's Cup analogy is a confining metaphorical envelope at its limits, it is nonetheless a good literary vehicle to exploit a cross-discipline synergy that otherwise might go unnoticed.

WHO'S WHO?

Professor Gould is 90 percent researcher and 10 percent ad specialty salesman. Mr. Danzig is 90 percent advertising-oriented journalist and 10 percent ad specialty buyer-recipient. Mr. Petisi is 90 percent ad specialty-premium consultant and 10 percent researcher-administrator.

The questions they have concerning promotional merchandise and their need for answers are very similar. Each wants answers for different reasons, however.

DANZIG'S DOSSIER

There is more to Fred Danzig than has been told so far. As editor of one of the most respected advertising trade journals, Mr. Danzig occupies a unique position in the ad specialty world of giveaways, geegaws, and gimmicks.

- He knows advertising, and his position keeps him at the forefront of the industry.

- He personally receives a higher than average number of ad specialties—"two or three a month, mostly from public relations people." They are used primarily to persuade him or his staff to cover a specific product or event. Many are part of an invitation to a press event. (Six have taken up permanent residence in his office.)
- He gives away ad specialties. A weekly reader contest called TNT (The Next Trend) has an imprinted T-shirt as the prize.
- *The Advertising Age* sales department uses ad specialties on a regular basis, and although he has no control of or involvement with this department, he knows whether or not its advertising efforts are successful.
- He is an observer of the ad specialty industry, and because the formal research pool is shallow and his knowledge of advertising deep, Mr. Danzig's observations carry substantial weight.

TNT Promotion Explodes

The case history applicable to the Reese's Cup Seminar is the use of promotional merchandise to support "The Next Trend" column.

"*Advertising Age* is 58 years old," Mr. Danzig says. "We look for ways to sustain interest and cement our relationship with our readers, because when you ask for [subscription] renewal, they are more apt to subscribe. One of the ways we do this is through features people respond to, and one of those features is 'The Next Trend' written by Lenore Skenazy."

"The Next Trend" is a weekly column that asks readers to identify the next trend in an industry. One week readers will be asked to name the next new allergy medicine, and then they will have to name the next Russian baseball or football team.

The ad specialty prize for the best entry is a black T-shirt of average quality that says "Advertising Age" on the back and "The Next Trend" on the front, in yellow letters.

The column is very popular, and "it is obvious that people and even departments spend a lot of time on an entry," Mr. Danzig says.

Michael Jackson Wins for John Eccleston

The first prize winner of the new allergy medicine name was John J. Eccleston, VP, Block Group, New York. His name: "Michael Jackson Signature Allergy Capsules: Wake up with a new nose." Second prize was "What's Your Signus? Formulated to match your astrological sign." It was submitted by Nick Barelli, executive VP, Ad Forces, Rockford, Illinois. Third prize went for "Poconose: A mountain of relief for a whole range of allergy symptoms," submitted by Bernard Falkoff, CEO, Bernard Falkoff Creative Services, Ardmore, Pennsylvania.

There is no question about how successful the feature is. Ms. Skenazy receives entries each week and prints about 20 "Honorable Intentions" in addition to the first, second, and third prize entries. The question is how effective is the T-shirt as a prize?

In addition, how do they know at *Advertising Age* that the T-shirt has any effect on the contest entries? Wouldn't creative types, spurred by the challenge of doing what they do best and the lure of national publicity, enter anyway?

Tell Us Your Shirt Size

"We don't think so," says Mr. Danzig. "We ask for your T-shirt size when you enter. Everyone tells us. If it didn't matter, they might not remember to give us their size." This fact is even more significant when you realize there is no form to fill out. It's not as easy as checking "L" or "XL" (the only sizes offered) on a printed entry form. Entrants are asked to submit pertinent information in an accompanying note.

"We also get letters from readers asking for a T-shirt because they have entered every contest—even though they haven't won yet. Some people ask us to send them two T-shirts if they win. There is a lot of conniving going on to get one. They are a status symbol."

But only, it seems, if you win one. An attempt to sell them through the magazine failed. "If you buy one, it doesn't mean as much," Mr. Danzig says.

But why a T-shirt? The selection came without undue research. "We like to see people wearing them. We are aiming at the younger readers who are more likely to wear T-shirts. Our audience for this column is made up of people who like wearing the T-shirts around the shop," Mr. Danzig says.

When asked how many imprinted T-shirts he personally owned, he estimated that 50 percent of his T-shirts are imprinted—a ratio he extrapolated to entrants in TNT. "They are a basic part of your wardrobe."

Economics Are with Us

The magazine spends about $1,500 a year on TNT T-shirts that "go out all over the country and give us tremendous visibility. The economics are all on the side of continuing to do it," Mr. Danzig adds.

There has been no specific follow-up research on the use or life of the TNT T-shirts. The column's popularity and the large number of entries is proof enough to the staff that the program is a success.

Still, the decision to use the T-shirt was based on what Dr. Gould calls "Advertising specialty buyers' perceptions of recipients' preferences for selected items." While Ad Age may be right on the money with its choice, you—a buyer—may not have the luxury of a staff of advertising-immersed professionals around you the next time you need to decide whether to buy a T-shirt or a tea cup.

Dr. Gould's study is a joint effort with Maria Tirelli, marketing coordinator of Computers for Construction, Ossining, New York. It incorporates an earlier study, "The $3 Billion Question," in which Dr. Gould and Timothy J. Hanlon, Jr., the eastern zone manager Food Service Division of Hills Brothers Coffee, Inc., Edgewater, New Jersey, investigate recipients' preferences for promotional items.

GETTING WHAT YOU WANT

A trade group, The Specialty Advertising Association International (SAAI), already had determined that the most frequently bought items were: writing instruments (17 percent of the total), wearables (14 percent), calendars (14 percent) and leather/vinyl goods (12 percent). Dr. Gould and Mr. Hanlon, however, wanted to see whether, if given the opportunity to choose, recipients would say "yes" to the same items in the same percentages—the equivalent of Mr. Danzig asking the winners if they wanted a T-shirt and the winners saying "yes."

The Gould-Hanlon study shows that *Advertising Age*'s T-shirt may not be the best giveaway. While wearables do account for 14 percent of ad specialty sales, not until they are offered in the $12 to $25 range are they a preferred item. Even then, they are in a dead heat with leather goods, a point behind housewares, and a point ahead of electronics. The important point here is that nobody believes the TNT T-shirt is in this price range. It falls into the $5 to $12 range of this study, and in this slot, it falls way back in popularity. Only 5 percent chose it, compared with 20 percent who chose electronics, 10 percent who chose housewares, and 7 percent each for pens and leather goods.

But the story is not told completely here. The Gould-Hanlon study ranked preferences by sex, and again the T-shirt took a beating. Seventeen percent of males, the highest preference, wanted electronics, and there was a three-way tie—16 percent of females wanted leather goods, housewares, and electronics. Wearables came in at 8 percent for males and 7 percent for females.

By age, the T-shirt fared better. Nearly half (48 percent) of the respondents between 30 and 39 preferred wearables. Between 40 and 49, the number dropped to 8 percent, and went steadily down until there was nothing but a blank space under the 60 to 69 column. Pens, electronics, and glass/ceramics enjoyed the most consistent preference across all ages.

Wearables rebounded in the education table with clothing the choice of 54 percent of college graduates. Electronics trailed by only two points.

The "Me" Geegaw Is Important

Interestingly, the personal identification category (something with a recipient's name or initials on it) skyrocketed with the college graduate group to 53 percent. The reason this is important is that preference for a personalized item did not show up in significant numbers in the other tables.

The income table showed that in the $30 to $59,000 column, calendars were most popular followed by pens, personalized items, electronic items, and then wearables. The actual numbers were close, but this also was the largest income group. Of these that showed strong in the $30 to $59,000 income level, only personalized items remained strong in the $60 to $99,000 column.

The preferences by occupation table has only one occupation—middle management—that could be paralleled to the audience participating in TNT. Of the people who liked wearables, 49 percent were middle managers, compared with 56 percent for those who liked personalized items. Calendars again showed up near the top with a 56 percent rating among middle managers.

Sports Wins

The table that covers hobbies shows that if you like sports, you overwhelmingly like promotional merchandise of all types. Reading, travel, gardening, crafts, and fishing fare substantially worse coming in with low double-digit and single-digit percents, while no product class is less than 60 percent among sports enthusiasts.

X-Out the T-Shirt

So what does this say about the selection of a T-shirt? That it probably isn't the best, but without data to the contrary, nobody would probably ever know because the contest itself is so creative, popular, and well managed. (Please see Acknowledgments note concerning Mr. Danzig.)

After studying the data, an alternate suggestion for a top prize would take into account the audience profile: college educated, earning between $30,000 and $59,000 a year, with some audience members in the $100,000 column, evenly split between male and female, probably conspicuous consumers.

This group's preferences for advertising specialties within the T-shirt price range of $5 to $12, according to the Gould-Hanlon study, show a high incidence of preference for personalized items, as well as the consistently high preference for pens and calendars.

Calendars Out

The choice between the two is relatively simple. First, calendars lose for two reasons: 1) Recipients request them often, and get them. They then choose the best and put the rest in a drawer or throw them away. 2) Neither a wall calendar nor a pocket calendar/appointment book would provide the best advertising reach for the magazine. They would either be on an office—or worse a kitchen—wall, or in someone's pocket or desk drawer. Additionally, while a pocket calendar could be personalized, a wall calendar would look stupid if it were personalized. (This study was conducted in June. If it had been conducted in November or December, when people think about calendars, they might have been a higher priority among respondents.)

Not Any Pen

This leaves the pen. Just any pen, however, will not work. If the average entrant has a choice of calendars, he or she has an unlimited supply of pens. Nevertheless, a special pen designed to achieve the following results would be—statistically—a success.

First, it must be clean, modern, of high quality, and inexpensive, but with a high perceived dollar value (something the T-shirt lacks).

Second, it must be able both to carry the contest logo as well as each winner's name and the contest name and to present itself as a complete graphics package.

Third, it has to reach *Advertising Age's* target audience and be flexible enough in its message to reinforce the magazine's primary advertising message.

Fourth, it has to be a status symbol and a conversation piece. Unlike the T-shirt, the pen could be "worn" to business meetings, around clients, and on job interviews—providing *Advertising Age* with exponentially more exposure, and the winner with an exponentially greater amount of status.

Parker Provides Prize

The pen that fits these criteria is the Parker™ Vector roller ball. It is a modern, plastic-covered metal pen with a prestigious nameplate. It comes in several colors and can be imprinted over 99 percent of its surface with up to five colors. Parker's silk-screening standards are among the highest in the world, ensuring a quality imprint on a quality writing instrument.

The plastic housing can be engraved in color, making it possible to add winners' names as well as contest names to each pen. The roller ball has a high perceived value, and it is refillable. This means the Advertising Age message will last as long as the pen, not as long as the ink.

Three Models

At one point, the T-shirts were offered for sale, but the effort failed. The pens could re-address this need to reach more people, without altering the exclusivity or status of the award. Unlike the T-shirt, which comes in only one model, the roller ball is available in several colors and styles. Model differentiation could be used to segregate winners and winning team members from runners-up, entrants, and readers. Three models could be created with variations in the graphics, engraving, or the color of the pen. This would allow an entire creative group to participate in the award, without reducing the status of the pen awarded to the member of that group who is declared the winner. A base-line model could be used by the advertising department space reps as a leave-behind during advertising sales calls. It too could be engraved, but with a media buyer's name.

Status Symbolic

The key to this distribution across several audience segments is model differentiation. Special care must be taken to ensure that each group retains its own measure of status.

This may guarantee a statistically favorable chance to success, but other considerations need to be discussed to increase the odds of the pen becoming a practical success. These considerations are graphics and introduction. The graphics on the new pen need to be evolutionary. People familiar with the current graphics should recognize the new version immediately and assume the changes are representative of the feature's success. The graphics should increase demand for the pen, just as the pen will increase demand over the T-shirt.

Models Featured

The introduction of the new models could be a feature in the magazine. The first model for winners, the story will explain, will include the name, finishing position, and contest name. The second model, a bit different, will have the same information and will be recognized as a collaborator's award. A photo of the pens will show the differences. Winners will be able to decide how many of each model they want. Advertising Age will not have to vary from its current policies of giving awards free to winners. If winners can get two T-shirts, they could get two pens.

SAFEGUARDING THE AWARD

Pens over the allotted limit, however, would be purchased. Purchasing TNT T-shirts is where the magazine got into trouble before; however, the following safeguards should eliminate any future problems: 1) Extra pens could only be purchased by the winner. He or she would order and receive them for the group. 2) The price would be set at less than retail, and the difference made up with Parker co-op advertising funds (their name will be used in the magazine); quantity discounts; and depending on the level of internal commitment, an *Advertising Age* co-op contribution.

With these safeguards in place, winners will have the flexibility to buy extra pens—one to put in a drawer for safekeeping, or one for a spouse. With the option always available, winners will feel more comfortable using their pens, knowing that if they are lost or broken, they can be replaced. This replacement option, too, will help keep the Ad Age name in front of its target audience for the long haul.

BASE LINE FOR BACK ROOM

The base line model will not be part of the introduction. It will be substantially different from the two primary models, used by the advertising department, and not directed at this audience. Further research will determine how it will be given out, and to whom. As mentioned before, it will be possible to engrave recipient's names on the base line model.

It might serve an additional function, if audience demand warrants. If entrants and other non-winners request pens in sufficient numbers, the base-line model could be offered. Similarly, if requests come in from former winners, the pens could be made available to them with appropriate engraving and at a fair price. These actions, however, must be audience-driven, and time-separated from the main introduction. This is not a revenue-generating program, nor is it primarily an advertising program, it is a recognition program. This message must be clear to the audience.

Computer Statistics on the Way

If Dr. Gould has his way, this process of finding the right merchandise for an ad specialty program will begin on a computer. As this book goes to press, he is working on ad specialty evaluation software. Using an IBM compatible computer, the user—in this case a promotional incentive item buyer—will feed in information and learn, pre-purchase, whether the item considered is likely to communicate a given message with a given audience. What we just went through with the TNT promotion theoretically could be done on a computer. A second part of the computer program is a post-purchase module that for the first time allows corporate buyers to measure the cost-effectiveness of promotional merchandise campaigns. Information entered into the computer for one incentive program is reused in new contexts when future promotional incentive programs are being considered. The cumulative effect of this body of statistical information will be to progressively fine-tune incentive media over an extended period of time.

Until then, however, Professor Gould relies on his graduate students and their willingness to help him carry out his research.

A CUTTY ABOVE

Mr. Petisi at Saatchi Saatchi Promotions doesn't have graduate students. He still relies on his feel for the industry; and, in the case of "Live A Cutty Above," he was right.

His group was charged with conceiving and implementing a promotional merchandise program to increase display incidence of Cutty Sark™ scotch. The program, as he defines it, "was skewed against a soft brown goods [scotch, bourbon] industry."

The store display showed garment bags, desk lamps, letter openers, and other premium premiums that were available free with purchase. The merchandise was upscale; targeted directly to scotch drinkers. The objectives: to leverage more display activity and support the new advertising position "Live A Cutty Above" were reached when the promotion increased display incidence 30 to 40 percent.

Although there are many similarities between the *Advertising Age* TNT promotion and the Cutty Sark effort with respect to choosing the right merchandise to support the effort, the merchandise in the Cutty Sark promotion drove the program, while the promotion drove the merchandise in the Ad Age case history. Knowing what role merchandise is to play in a promotion is one of the keys to using merchandise correctly. Some people, recognizing the tremendous power of promotional incentive items, are reckless in their choices, but successful nonetheless.

Together, Dr. Gould's studies and the two case histories show that you—the buyer—can statistically determine what your audience wants, and then add your own practical knowledge of your audience to come up with the right merchandise.

CHAPTER 7

USING AN AGENT

Agents are like abacuses: invaluable if you know how to use them. If you don't, you could easily go through life wondering why anyone would bother with one.

Agents are not a necessity, but they are endemic to the market. You do not need an agent to buy premiums or ad specialties. If you have a current edition of the *New York City Business to Business Yellow Pages* (all five boroughs), you can locate sufficient products to fulfill nearly any promotional merchandise program. There is a popular saying in New York that no matter how different, off-beat, or certifiably crazy someone is, there are five identical people in Greenwich Village. The same analogy can be used for merchandise. Using the aforementioned *Yellow Pages,* you should be able to find at least five suppliers of any particular item you have in mind. The suppliers may not all speak English, but they are eager to do business nonetheless. (For some unknown reason, there is an abundance of ad specialty suppliers in Minnesota—primarily Minneapolis and suburbs—so a business to business yellow pages might be useful for this locale, too. Here, however, most speak English, although Bostonians might argue the point.)

Sourcing through the Yellow Pages, though, does not necessarily mean you are buying directly from the manufacturer—bypassing the middleman. You could be dealing with the rep, agent, or other intermediary who may warehouse the product or may just take the orders and ask the factory to ship the goods. You also may find yourself dealing directly with the president of the manufacturing firm from which you purchase products, and so you are convinced you are dealing "directly" and getting the lowest price. The president, however, without telling you, may be paying a loyal local agent a commission on your purchases. Unlike the Cheshire cat in *Alice in Wonderland*, you can't always see the smile on the face of the invisible participating agent.

Whether all this makes any difference depends on your requirements and the price you are willing to pay for the goods as well as the agent's services. In the case of the "Cheshire agent," you are paying, unknowingly, for a service you are not receiving. There can be situations, however, when your price is sufficiently low so that you don't care what unknown agent gets a cut. You want the peace of mind you get dealing directly with the factory.

WHAT AGENTS DO

So, if you don't need an agent to get access to products, what do agents do for you? A short story first:

There was a time when business people played a game of one-upmanship, challenging each other to determine exactly what business certain corporations were engaged in. The uninitiated to the game would say McDonald's Corporation is in the hamburger business. Untrue would say the one-upmen. McDonald's is in the real estate business. It owns the ground each franchise sits on. It is real estate that the bankers ask for when they want loan collateral, not Quarter Pounders™, and on and on.

Applying the same rules, agents don't buy and sell goods, they worry. They're in the worrying business. If they aren't good worriers, they aren't good agents.

A good agent/worrier knows the reality of the business is that the order is going to get screwed up. Limiting the damage, making shrewd compromises, continually renegotiating with suppliers and keeping you worry-free are the behind-the-scenes activities of a good agent.

There aren't many good agents. This particular talent is not a taught skill. How many times have you heard that the pens are going to take another two weeks, the color is off on the T-shirts, the supplier substituted polyester jackets for cotton? The common occurrence of these mundane excuses is evidence of the small universe of good agents. Because when you are using an agent, problems are never the manufacturer's fault. They're the agent's fault. The agent chose the manufacturer. If you buy merchandise directly from the manufacturer, and there is a screw-up, of course it is the manufacturer's fault. But when you place an agent in the middle, that person is the one whose job description mandates moving closer to the fan when whatever starts hitting it.

"STUDY GEEGAWS, SON"

Additionally, the cadre of good agents is small because the reward pool is relatively shallow. The mentors in the overstuffed chairs at the Princeton Club don't say to their protegees, "study geegaws."

It is not a profession an aspiring young college student necessarily prepares for, even if one were convinced it held the monetary rewards equal to those in investment banking or insider trading. It is a profession into which many average salespeople end up, some lucky ones land, and a few good people gravitate. There are a lot of lottery players looking for the million key tag order from the beer company; a lot of part-timers with a desk and phone in the basement, and a lot of one-account one-man operations existing by the favor of the buyer and a bold-face blurb in the phone book under "Advertising Specialties."

The successful ones, however, find their niche among buyers who understand the abacus-like nature of the calling. In fact, this understanding of what each can do for the other is the most important criteria in a successful buyer-agent relationship. Put another way, when the agent knows what and what not to worry about, the relationship is well-defined.

Since it takes little preparation or insight to handle a promotional merchandise agent badly, the following section will concentrate on how, with preparation, this agent-buyer relationship can be structured to benefit each party.

As a buyer, you must know what you want your agent to do for you. Because many agents are one- or two-man bands, they won't deliver on all the duties listed below. You probably don't want them to. Determine which are most important to you, and include them in an agent's contract which you both sign.

If you, the buyer, can accurately define your needs, you will find the right agent.

First, the agent must be a salesperson—a good order-taker obsessed with detail. This person is in the business of selling you custom-made products. This person is not your lawyer, your accountant, or your hair dresser. Again and again, surveys show the majority of promotional merchandise buyers want a good salesperson, not a marketing or creative genius. They give the order to someone who will deliver the goods at the right price.

With this foundation, the following are several other attributes you may need in an agent. These needs may change depending on the merchandise you want to buy or the communications program in which the merchandise will be used, so you may find yourself with two or three specialized agents you call on for specific tasks.

MARKETING SAVVY

How much promotional merchandise-directed marketing savvy will you demand of your agent? If you say, "I want 250 Parker Jotters(TM) for the sales conference," you need an agent/order-taker. Don't look for Procter & Gamble marketing experience on the resume and don't pay for it if it's there. If you ask for your agent's opinion: "What should we give away at the sales conference?" you still don't need a P&G alumnus, but you could use someone with a good feel for what role merchandise plays in your company's environment, and for what's available. For whatever reasons—ego, low self-esteem, or an unrealistic view of their role in business—many agents see themselves as marketing geniuses. If you don't need this genius, real or imagined, screen out these agents early in your selection process.

ART AND LAYOUT CAPABILITIES

If you are the type of buyer who sketches your ad specialty imprint ideas on a Post-It Note(TM) and leaves the rest to chance, you need an agent with art and layout capabilities. Unfortunately, most merchandise order-taking agents are not sensitive to the importance of good art. Many will say they can handle art preparation, but many have only the most elementary knowledge of layout, mechanicals, color, and typography. A corporate identity book sends them reeling. Manufacturers are often worse. They do not appreciate your logo and generally think nothing of shrinking it, re-coloring it, tilting it, or reversing it. This doesn't mean they will change a 7-Eleven Food Stores logo to 18, but their liberties with logos is legend.

If you need art and layout service, ask your agent for it, and be ready to pay for it. It is a service that cannot legitimately come out of an agent's profit. The art, the message, and its placement and production quality are the greatest single contributor to the appeal and acceptance of the finished merchandise. Many relationships between agents and buyers have soured because of poorly produced art that manufacturers used anyway to manufacture unacceptable merchandise.

CREATIVITY

Here again, many sales-oriented agents come up with a case of the shorts. But they're not the only ones. There is no watershed of promotional merchandise creativity concentrated in corporations. Else, why do so many insurance companies give away the same tired pens year after year—cheap ones at that.

To be useful to your organization in a creative sense, the merchandise agent has to understand you, your company culture, your needs, and how the three can be combined in a product that will be acceptable. This is asking a lot. Agents can meet you halfway by knowing the products they sell and how to get the message you request across most effectively. For instance, you may want someone who can creatively imprint a special event logo on hats. You have created the logo and chosen the hats. The agent can then find the best way to get the message across. With respect to promotional merchandise, creativity is like coffee and curry—the scent of it often is more enticing than the real thing. Measured doses of creativity as well as curry go a long way. Cute, clever, dramatic, and different often describe merchandise that effectively overpowered the message it was created to carry.

A GOOD NEGOTIATOR

Some buyers feel they're not getting their money's worth unless they can see haggling going on with the manufacturer. Many of this type are from the purchasing side of the corporation; and if you are one, find an agent whose surrogate negotiating powers inspire confidence. Most of the time, however, if you're an active buyer you'll go directly to the source of the haggling and have marginal use for agents. If you have an aversion to the Baghdad-Flea-Market atmosphere surrounding the purchase of promotional merchandise, you should get an agent because negotiating must take place. You may need special help with price, delivery, special imprinting, or hard-to-get merchandise. And at these times, having a good negotiator on your side who understands the process as it relates to merchandise can make you a very happy person.

Negotiating is an ethereal ability you usually can't recognize in an agent until you've committed to working with the person. Evidence of it early on comes in several forms. First, a good negotiator will rarely say no when you ask for something a little different, or a little quicker, or a little less expensive. These requests from you are the key phrases that signal the opportunity to use their negotiating talent. Although the good negotiator will rarely say no to a request, he or she might not say yes, either. Instead, you'll get a round of questions asked to help define your negotiating parameters so these can be used when dealing with the manufacturer.

Another way to recognize a good negotiator—especially if you recognize that you are not—is that the person will embrace the chance to haggle while you will get a knot in your stomach. Be careful to recognize that this talent, as with others, needs to be rewarded—paid for. When you want your agent to negotiate price, do not automatically expect that the agent's profit is fair game for reduction. If you do, you're not looking for a negotiator, you're looking for a patsy. Patsies are out there, but they don't live in negotiator's bodies.

IN-DEPTH PRODUCT KNOWLEDGE

A typical agent has access to hundreds of thousands of products and can't know much about all of them. If you demand in-depth knowledge from your agent, narrow the product categories so it will be humanly possible to attain this product knowledge. If your company's emphasis is on wearables—shirts, jackets and caps—it is reasonable to ask that your agent be an expert in this part of the business with respect to styles, manufacturer inventories and close-outs, prices, and imprinting. If, however, you know exactly what you want, find an agent who is a good order taker/worrier and save yourself the money you will pay for an agent with product knowledge.

PROFESSIONALLY-AFFILIATED AGENT

Depending on what merchandise you need, an agent's membership in organizations may help you get better pricing and better selection. The largest of these merchandise organizations is the Advertising Specialty Institute (ASI) in Langhorne, Pennsylvania, a for-profit corporation self-described as a publishing company—just as McDonald's Corporation is a real estate company. ASI is in reality a grand matchmaker for member manufacturers and agents. It produces directories for agents that show product, pricing and the whereabouts of ad specialties. The agent then calls the manufacturer who sends a standardized catalog—with an agent's mark-up included in coded pricing—which the buyer peruses. These catalogs have no address or phone number, preventing buyers from bypassing the agent and going directly to the manufacturer.

For manufacturers, ASI produces lists of agents and their respective credit records. The two—manufacturer and agent—meet by purchase order and commerce happens. Some manufacturers declare that they will only sell through agents belonging to ASI, others say they will only deal with agents, regardless of their ASI affiliation, not end users. In any case many agents do not belong to ASI, and many ASI suppliers work directly with end users.

If you are a frequent buyer of giveaways, geegaws, gimmicks, doodads, and freebies—the classic ad specialty—your agent will be able to serve you better if he or she belongs to ASI. The firm specializes in categorizing this type of merchandise.

FACTORY REPS

If, however, your purchases tend more towards toaster ovens, electric shavers, television sets, and other consumer goods—the classic premiums—an ASI-affiliated agent will be of little help. You might want to look for an agent who is a direct factory rep of several lines of products you might use. If you work in or around New York City, reps usually cannot give you the most competitive pricing on this type of merchandise, even though they deal directly with the factory. To get the best price, you can purchase the goods from retail discount stores. But, you may not want to unless price is your only consideration. The reason is service. If you need small quantities of the product drop shipped over a period of time, or if you don't want to negotiate with a teenage TV salesman at Nutty Larry's while Van Halen screams in the background, you can call an agent and let him or her do your worrying.

If you live outside the northeast, agents who are factory reps probably are your best bet from a pricing standpoint, but check the local discount stores anyway if you have that do-it-yourself bent.

Agents who are factory reps generally do not carry any inventory or handle competing brands. They are order-takers in the truest sense of the term. The manufacturer invoices your company and pays the rep a commission after it receives your check. Reps usually work through the premium incentive division of the company, not the retail sales division. The result of this alternate placement on the organization chart is that premium reps do not participate in the best pricing programs. This is why you often can get the television set or the ice cream maker cheaper at a retail discount store.

Unlike the freebies, geegaws, and doodads purchases—where you probably won't know who the manufacturer is, it is obvious who manufactures the microwave oven you buy for your merchandise program. Because of your ability to go directly to the retail manufacturers, most protect their rep's commissions by telling you that the price they quote already has the rep's commission in it whether you use the rep or not. This is not necessarily true, especially when the numbers get big. With competing products—say a half million coolers—where three or four manufacturers could produce similar versions, price becomes very important. The price paring usually starts with the rep's commission, and the shakedown comes from the manufacturer who realizes that you, the buyer, don't usually care about the internal machinations involved in producing a better price. The best way to sidestep what is obviously an unethical—but very common—practice is to decide on your actions before you call a rep. If you know that you will be placing a large order that will be competitively bid, call the company directly first. Explain that you do not need the services of a rep, and that you plan to ask for competitive bids. Punctuate the fact that price will be a determining factor. Declare that you have called no rep yet, and if the manufacturer wants to work directly with you—compensating its rep in any way it feels is fair—then you are amenable. If the company says it prefers to work through its rep organization, then at least you have made your intentions clear. When the rep shows up, tell him or her exactly what you have done. The rep, seeing a completely unsolicited large order coming through the door, may initiate negotiations for a lower commission with the factory and pass the savings on to you.

Knowing the facts up front will allow the factory and the reps to give you what you want—in this case the lowest price.

ASSOCIATIONS

Other agent affiliations range from social to lobbying-oriented—including local, regional, and national groups that put on trade shows, provide member services, and dispense awards. Overall, the industry is fragmented and suffers from negative image problems. One of the largest associations, The Specialty Advertising Association International (SAAI) headquartered in Dallas, decided a few years ago to forego a serious image campaign in favor of paying off the association headquarters. The message was clear when they diverted funds from member activities, that their primary business is real estate, not the promotion of the advertising specialty business. The fact that the members didn't seem to mind further states the case that the industry is fragmented and loosely defined with no clear direction. Using the same general description, you'll find good salespeople and bad consultants, good idea people and bad implementers. Any association that claims to represent more than 100 promotional merchandise agents on any subject that affects their pocketbook, is dreaming.

FREIGHT FORWARDER & WAREHOUSER

If you know what you want and what you want is overseas, you may want an agent with a specialty in freight forwarding. Often the trickiest part of getting the merchandise from Taiwan or Hong Kong is getting it here on time. Overseas buying means you probably are purchasing large quantities of merchandise, and so you may need an agent with a warehouse. Promotional merchandise tends to grow legs when it is stored in corporate supply rooms, so keeping it out of reach means less responsibility and possible extended payment terms if you can get your agent to invoice you only when you take delivery of the merchandise.

Although you are looking for a freight forwarder, you first need a promotional merchandise agent. Any freight forwarder is not good enough. A merchandise agent with a specialty in freight forwarding can give you valuable information that will affect the success of your promotional merchandise program. For example, Swiss factories close down during July. If you're waiting for your Swiss Army knives, the blooms will be off the crocuses before you see them because when the factory reopens, it always is swamped with orders.

TO CONCEAL YOUR IDENTITY

Take yourself out of your buyer's chair for a moment and consider this: If you were manufacturing a particular geegaw and a buyer from a Fortune 100 company who looked just like you wanted to buy 200 geegaws for delivery next Thursday, would you consider nudging the price skyward in the name of a rush charge because the company obviously could afford it and the market would bear it?

If you answered no to this question, find yourself a good bankruptcy lawyer before you decide to go into ad specialty manufacturing, because you won't be in business long. Like a sea gull plumbs a landfill, so will an astute geegaw manufacturer plumb a corporate piggy bank, and here is where an agent can help you immeasurably. With an agent as your intermediary, the manufacturer doesn't know whether the order for 200 imprinted fly swatters is for Saint Mary's Church or St. Regis Paper. Once your agent determines the best manufacturer, he or she can submit the artwork, permitting the end user to be known; but at this point, a good purchase order makes it too late to change pricing.

Keeping your identity a secret until the order is completely negotiated with a supplier also allows you to shop the market without enduring the weeks of follow-up calls stimulated by your corporate name. For whatever reason, if Jim's Auto Body Shop calls around for prices on 500 soft-feel key tags it won't generate nearly the excitement as if a billion dollar corporation middle manager makes the same call. The supposition is that the billion dollar corporation will buy more merchandise, but there is a finite equation involved in Jim's Auto Body ad specialty purchases. So, as the buyer, your phone rings off the hook. It won't happen if your agent makes these calls.

CASH FLOW CUSHION

Many agents ask for money up front to cover orders. Many buyers regularly pay agents nothing up front and hold off paying for goods long after they have been delivered. If you want to use your agent as a cash flow cushion: "Don't bill me for this until after the fiscal year," negotiate it up front. Conversely, if you discuss up-front payments with your agent, you could be easing his cash flow with payment before delivery. It's no secret that a lot of agents are financially pinched. This doesn't necessarily mean you shouldn't deal with them. It means you should talk about the transference of money before you get into your first deal. Maybe your agent is willing to settle for less profit, if you will pay up front or at delivery. Maybe, too, you want to find an agent who won't dun you for being 90 days late.

A lot of manufacturers demand money up front. They want to make sure that when the merchandise is delivered with a mistake, the agent and end user have something to lose, too. Smart agents will keep your money and their own free from this kind of extortive encumbrance as much as possible. If you agree to pay money up front, make sure that should the mistake be unfixable, you retain the flexibility to back out of the deal. While no reasonable person enters into a purchase agreement with the express purpose of finding an excuse to back out, you may want to back out. If you have money on the table, your backing out may be painful.

TYPES OF AGENTS

What about the different types of agents? With respect to the different talents of each individual agent, they all tend to fall into three groups:

- Incentive Slaves.
- Restricted, Registered, and Pedigreed.
- Aliases.
- Free Agents.

Incentive Slaves

Like most sales departments, those of ad specialty and premium manufacturers regularly hold sales incentive contests. Some agents take these contests more seriously than others. For some, the journey from sanity to incentive slave is a short one. A dead giveaway that your agent is an incentive slave is that no matter what you want, somehow the same product keeps popping up as the "perfect merchandise." About the third time this happens, you begin to realize that the agent needs adult supervision. He or she will come into your office with the subject merchandise, personalized with your name and company logo already on it, and proceed to find a way to make it fit into your program. Six weeks later, when the perfect giveaways arrive—in the wrong color—your incentive slave is bobbing on a jet ski at Myrtle Beach. One classic incentive slave peddled non-spill coffee mugs for a mediocre cruise to the Caribbean. These were the inverted cone-shaped ugly cups that you could drink from only if you had a face like an anteater. Normally-lipped humans found the non-spill mug was also non-functional. You needed the non-medical equivalent of a proctoscope to look inside the mug to see if it was clean. They were popular for about nine months—long enough for clear-headed people to realize that these annoyances were truly unneeded, even in the geegaw world. Nevertheless every time a customer would ask for promotional merchandise suggestions, the incentive slave would dust off the non-spill coffee mug. This agent sold more than 40,000 of them.

Restricted, Registered and Pedigreed

Manufacturers love these agents. Contracts and other agreements abound, giving the agent all manner of territorial rights, favorable pricing, and special status with the home office.

Agents waste no time letting you know that they are the only authorized dealer of Product Number 5, or Klink-Klank pens. The smart ones also waste no time giving you the list price of the item and smugly sit back waiting for you to buy. This type of agent can do you no good unless you demand the overpriced products he or she sells. They spend their waking hours peddling the products they exclusively handle. The successful ones with exclusive territories tend to get lazy, and the unsuccessful ones get tired of pitching the same old product, regardless of need. Either way, they interrupt the normal competitive atmosphere of the promotional merchandise business, and the corporation writing the check is forced to add more zeroes than it should to pay for these exclusive products.

Aliases

The Beatles song "Rocky Racoon" has a line: "Her name was McGill, she called herself Lil, but everyone knew her as Nancy."

There are many nom-de-merchandise businesses, too. Your advertising agency, sales promotion house, public relations firm, marketing consultant, personnel group can all be aliases for promotional merchandise sellers. All these entities at one time or another recommend purchasing merchandise—usually in conjunction with a program within their discipline. In these cases the aliases are acting as your "Lil" even though you know them as "Nancy." They are notoriously naive when it comes to buying the merchandise. In fact, they are the reason there are retail prices. And, these aliases regularly mark-up these retail prices before sending you the invoice.

In their defense, these aliases are usually the only ones who attempt to integrate the merchandise into a campaign, but most of them don't know the first thing about the purchasing and manufacturing side of the business. If you are faced with this situation, recommend the alias use your agent and isolate the billing from the alias by having your agent handle it. The important thing to remember is that if you do not take action, you will be paying more than you should. You have to make it clear that you are not trying to take money away from the alias, but trying to save your corporation money. As a fall-back position, it is cheaper to pay the alias a consulting fee equal to what they would have made on the marked-up merchandise than to pay the inflated merchandise prices. Your agent will be able to get the products cheaper, and so you will have saved money without losing the services of your alias or your agent.

Free Agent

As the name implies, this is the agent who is philosophically positioned to have your interest at heart. He or she is successful when what you want is supplied. A free agent doesn't have to spend a lot of time cajoling you into buying something you don't want, and when it comes time to take a vacation, you won't have unknowingly paid for it. Most free agents—when faced with customers who want a restricted product—have their own supply lines, and often, because they don't rely on this restricted product for the majority of their income, will be willing to discount it. Unlike the restricted agents, free agents will purchase any brand of can opener for you, not the one they happen to be repping. Most restricted, registered, and pedigreed agents don't like free agents. Some refuse to work with them. Stay away from these cat fights. If free agents can't fend for themselves, they won't be a free agent long. Some free agents can become demanding, insisting that you give them all your business or pay them for the research time they spend regardless of how much they may eventually mark up a product. If you think your free agent is worth it, pay the freight. Many buyers do. If he or she is good—able to work with your management, outside agencies, find merchandise you like, handle the odd one-of-a-kind product—you will see the value.

DISCOUNTS & PROFIT

This brings us to the profit part of the chapter. Should you know how much money your agent is making? The answer is simple. If you want to know, you should know.

In another chapter, alternatives to the traditional agent-company relationship are examined where you, the buyer, work with the agent to set fees and commissions. Corporations usually know how much their ad agencies make, how much their public relations firms, outside accountants, and lawyers make. Why not the promotional merchandise agent?

Many agents will tell you they want to keep their profit margins secret. This is not a gentlemen's business, and a dollar shaved is a dollar saved, no matter whose pocket it comes from. If you are the type of buyer who can't stand to see an agent make a profit, the kind who thinks agents somehow don't need money to live, then maybe you're better off not knowing what the gross margins are. Like most profit numbers, those of agents seem unreasonably high when you first see them—providing you see the real numbers. You may say sarcastically, "Here's a guy whose only expense is running the Steam-Away™ over the polyester suit once a month, and he's making this much on my order? I'll put a stop to this." The next time you see him, you are determined to cut his take, so you come up with a transparent story about your budgets being cut and how—temporarily—you need him to "work with you" for a couple months.

The agents see right through this. They understand your inability to respect their right to make a profit, and the smart ones will stop serving you. Your office will be overrun with the agents who can survive on your stingy budgets, and your promotional merchandise quality will reflect your "temporary" budget cuts.

It's far better to either remain in the dark about your agent's profit margins, or bypass the agent altogether and do the buying yourself. Using an agent means paying an agent, and as with everything, you get the services you are willing to pay for. Rather than expending energy finding ways to short-circuit an agent, discover ways to improve your buying procedures using your agent as a team member.

CHAPTER 8

BUY IT RIGHT AND AT THE RIGHT PRICE: THE CASE FOR A NEW TYPE OF CENTRALIZED PURCHASING

If you are one of those buyers who wonders why there are so many middle men in the promotional merchandise business or why the cheapest products at a retail store—styrofoam cups for example—seem to cost so much when they become "promotional merchandise," then you may want to consider some form of a centralized purchasing program for your company.

This chapter will show you how to determine whether your company can benefit from centralized purchasing, how to propose the program to your management, and how to implement it. It also will tell you what a centralized program is and is not, and how your new promotional merchandise agency will be part of your centralized purchasing team.

Before you read further, however, please understand that the program detailed here is a radically different approach to purchasing promotional merchandise. It is not as simple as figuring out how to buy directly from manufacturers—although from a price standpoint you will be doing just that. You will also need to understand that this centralized purchasing program requires a level of commitment from your management that may not usually be accorded the promotional merchandise buying function.

NO FREE FREEBIES

Americans hear after each election when it is time to talk about raising taxes—"There is no free lunch." The same is true with a centralized purchasing program. You will pay a fair wholesale price—never retail or catalog. You also will pay for the consultation, order trafficking, hand holding, and reporting that your promotional merchandise agency does. Even paying your agency, you will save money and enjoy the other benefits of the program, however. How much money you save, and how well you use the other built-in benefits depends on your ability to program, your management skill, your company's commitment, and your agency's abilities.

CAN YOU BENEFIT?

Here is the type of company or department that can benefit from this centralized purchasing program:

- A company whose promotional merchandise purchases are $50,000 a year or more purchased through reps, agents, and middlemen at retail or close to catalog prices.
- A company that has several people or departments individually purchasing similar products. For example, the personnel department may be buying anniversary pins, retirement gifts, or motivational or safety program merchandise. The sales and marketing department may be buying sales motivation and recognition products. The company sports teams buy uniforms. Everybody buys calendars and appointment books. Somebody is buying decals, binders, stickers, name tags, name plates, holiday greeting cards, and executive gifts.
- A company or department that is willing to consolidate the purchasing function with a promotional merchandise agency. This means the personnel department, the sales group, the plant department, the field offices, and the sports teams still do their own buying, but they buy through the official promotional merchandise agency.

• A company that wants control over what type of promotional merchandise is bought, wants to specify how the logo is displayed on this merchandise, and wants to know how target audiences react to the merchandise.
• A company seriously interested in tracking and controlling expenses.

This last point is included because promotional merchandise often is the largest untracked expenditure in a corporation. There are budgets for traditional advertising, promotion, office supplies, and virtually every other expense item, but promotional merchandise seems to slip through the seams of the budget. In many cases this represents substantial slippage.

ARE YOU MY TYPE?

The first step in an audition for a movie or a play is when actors are "typed out." The casting director—looking for a certain physical feature, tells all those actors lacking the needed feature, "Thank you." This means, "Please leave. We don't need you. You've been 'typed out.' "

You can "type in" your own company with respect to a centralized purchasing program if:

• Your management will listen to your ideas, and you have enough respect within your organization to make the case for centralized purchasing.
• You think it would be easier if an expert were able to handle this work for you for less money than you would spend handling—or mishandling it—by yourself.
• You now purchase promotional merchandise from long-time friends, lodge buddies, brothers, or brothers-in-law and are willing to look at a better way to buy.
• The promotional merchandise purchasing function is clean—no bribes, kick-backs, or free trips to Europe.

If you qualify, consider the following centralized purchasing concept:

- Your company or department will enter into a contract with a reputable, knowledgeable, and professional promotional merchandise agency to handle your promotional merchandise account.
- The agency would have equal stature with your accounting firm, advertising agency, public relations consultants, and outside legal advisors.
- This agency will sell your company or department all promotional merchandise at cost—including rebates, cumulative quantity discounts and all other current or future discounts.
- This agency will bill your company a negotiated monthly fee for hours spent servicing your account, for art work produced, and for travel and expenses incurred on your behalf.
- You will commit to a promotional merchandise budget for a specified period of time—usually one year—and you will allow your agency to begin planning and implementation of a program you both agree on which utilizes that budget.

NOTHING NEW

Law firms, accounting firms, and advertising and public relations agencies have worked under these same basic negotiated terms for years. Promotional merchandise firms, however, haven't caught on. More importantly, corporations have not yet realized that they can save thousands and hundreds of thousands of dollars by dealing this way with promotional merchandise firms.

Here is why the dollar savings are so significant. Promotional merchandise firms traditionally charge as if they were performing piece work. They do this because at best they can expect future business from you, but usually they have no idea how much business may be coming their way. At worst, you may never call them again regardless of how good the pricing or service on your last order was. This means promotional merchandise agencies cannot staff up—or down—to handle your needs. So, you pay the equivalent of full retail for what you buy every time you buy, unless you beat them up over price. In this case, you get a cheap price and no service.

DATE BUT NO MARRIAGE

In addition, you may use the research services of your ad specialty or premium rep and purchase nothing. The next time you buy from this person, he or she will recover those expenses, and this recovery will be reflected in your prices. Even if you didn't run your rep ragged without a resulting order, you may be picking up the tab for the last near-customer who did.

Under the terms of your centralized purchase agreement, you will tell your agency how much you are going to spend and what you require in terms of service. The agency will staff up to handle your account. You and the agency will negotiate a fee to cover the work performed, and the agency will sell you all merchandise at its cost.

LIKE OPENING A SAVINGS ACCOUNT

But how substantial are the savings? Take a common item such as a twill (no mesh on the back) baseball cap. An average wholesale price unimprinted is $1.90 (1988 dollars.) The wholesale total for 5,000 caps is $9,500. How much did you pay the last time you bought caps? Probably you don't know what you paid for the cap alone. The price included the silk screen, the embroidery or the patch glued on. Here is where you begin to realize the hidden benefits of a centralized purchasing program. Probably for the first time, you will be able to decide, without markups, whether you can really afford "expensive" embroidery, or cheaper silk screening, or patches, because you will see exactly what these items cost. It takes no more time to order 5,000 caps with embroidery than it does with silk screened imprints. However, because embroidery is more expensive, this extra cost is marked up along with the hat, exaggerating its true cost.

Let's suppose your agent is being kind and only marks up the $1.90 caps 35 percent. Before doing this, 35 cents is added to the $1.90 for a two-color silk screened imprint. This brings the cost to $3.04 per cap, or $15,200. Your agent has paid $11,250 for the caps and has made $3,950 profit.

Now let's suppose your agent spends three hours ordering, trafficking, and invoicing your hats. Your agent has made more than $1,300 per hour for work on your behalf.

GET ME MY GUN

Before you shoot your agent, realize that he or she does not spend all day placing orders at $1,300 per hour. Promotional merchandise agents as a group are not wealthy and their companies are not large. There are a few wealthy ones, but most are barely comfortable, less than 10-person organizations who are scrapping for sales.

The important point here is that you paid your agent more than $1,300 an hour for a three-hour job—$3,950—when, under the right circumstances, your agent would gladly work for much less, and provide additional services.

You can produce these "right circumstances" and take advantage of better pricing and better service.

These "right circumstances" mean consistent, planned sales. What you are saying to your agent is that he or she will agree to make a negotiated profit on your business for a negotiated level of service.

PROGRAM'S OTHER BENEFITS

Imagine, if you can, getting a call from your promotional merchandise agency account executive that is not a hard-sell call, but a service call. Imagine getting a meeting report, a program. Imagine getting a summary of sales by month, quarter; by department, or group. Imagine discussing the pros and cons of promotional merchandise without your agent being controlled by a hidden profit agenda. Imagine paying for what you get, not just paying.

PROFIT, PROFIT, WHERE'S THE PROFIT?

The previous sentence about a hidden profit agenda deserves to be more fully explained. Whether you know it or not, there are compelling profit motivations behind the products your ad specialty or premium rep offers you. These motivations range from varying markups agents receive when they sell products from a catalog with printed pricing to rebates, trips, free merchandise (for which you are charged), and higher quantity pricing.

DANCING FOR DOLLARS

As a buyer, you have a right to know what the motivations are. What an agent may portray as the perfect merchandise for your needs may instead be the perfect answer to his or her dreams of winning a suppliers' sales contest. Merchandise recommendations may also be made on the basis on printed catalog prices. For a competitive product such as coffee mugs, manufacturers will print catalogs with pricing that includes 80 to 100 percent markups for the agent. You will be restricted to those high-markup catalogs when you ask for a mug, even though a different mug with a lower profit margin may be what you need. Obviously, with a centralized purchasing program, you will avoid all this price tag tap dancing.

WHEN IS A HALF NOT A HALF?

As a buyer, you also have a right to know about up-front payments. When you are asked for a deposit, is it because the supplier asked the agent for a deposit or because the agent wants partial payment in advance? If the supplier asks for one-half up front, and the agent asks you for one-half up front, you probably are paying for the entire wholesale cost of the order. The agent can then use your money until the supplier's invoice comes due. There is nothing wrong with this, but you should be allowed to negotiate this practice and take normal discounts for early payment. Under the centralized purchasing program, you will have this flexibility. And, when a supplier wants half up front, that's all you will pay. You won't be unknowingly giving the agent his profit up front because his profit does not come from the merchandise sale.

SLICE THROUGH THE MIDDLEMAN

It is also important for buyers to know who the supplier is. Many agents keep this knowledge secret, and keep buyers from understanding the business. If you as the buyer can discuss your needs with a supplier or tour the plant, you can better understand problems, limitations, and opportunities in your promotional merchandise program. Think of the last time you received a shipment of merchandise that wasn't what you thought it would be. If you had better communications with the supplier, you would understand better why things turn out the way they do.

How many times, too, have you wished you could get that supplier on the phone and negotiate directly with him? Now you can. Maybe the negotiation takes the form of an invitation to the supplier to visit your offices where you schmooze for that best price—you and your agency double teaming him.

HOW YOUR AGENCY MAKES MONEY

The basic format—which you will fine-tune during your negotiations—is an hourly rate billed against an annual budget. Your agency, in its written and oral presentation to you, will estimate the time necessary to implement your program. This time will be billed on a monthly basis, justified with an activity report detailing work done. The cost of the merchandise is budgeted in the program, too. Your company can accept and pay invoices for merchandise—allowing you to continuously audit costs—or your agency can bill you net for merchandise with receipt backup. Other expenses such as travel to your offices, telephone calls, fax, copies, travel to trade shows, and other account-oriented and out-of-pocket expenses can be negotiated.

Your agency can amortize the projected consulting budget over 12 months and bill it in equal installments regardless of the actual hours logged against the account, or they can front- or back-load the billing depending on the seasonal nature of your promotional needs.

COST-PLUS AGREEMENTS

You may also want to enter into a cost-plus agreement with your agency. This contract allows the agency to recoup only its actual net overhead for servicing your account. Your agency's profit comes from a negotiated percent override on net sales. You would want this arrangement if many different departments were participating, and your management wanted each to pay its own share of expenses. Usually headquarters picks up the actual overhead and allocates it equally to all participating departments, and then each department picks up net costs plus negotiated profit. As with rental car companies, the markup to all departments can be reduced as your company reaches sales quotas. This way all departments can benefit from the purchases of a large department—a concept unheard of in the promotional merchandise business.

OTHER BENEFITS

State sales tax is usually not charged for consulting fees, and the monthly retainer is a legitimate consulting fee. This can amount to a substantial savings.

Your promotional merchandise agency can begin to work with corporate identity, advertising, public relations, sales, personnel, plant, and other groups on a regular basis. This consistent exposure to your company will become one of the most valuable assets of your relationship. Your agency will be able to meet your needs with greater accuracy and with greater efficiency.

QUESTIONS & ANSWERS

1. The guy I buy my promotional merchandise from couldn't begin to handle this kind of responsibility. He is a salesman. How do I find a promotional merchandise agency?

At the time of publication, Clay Clay Steven & Blair is the only agency handling this type of business. We pioneered the concept, borrowing on experience managing public relations accounts under the same terms. Larger agencies often have the capability, but usually are unwilling to let loose of the fat profit margins they enjoy from current customers. Small agencies that would like the business can't handle it. The concept is becoming more widespread, however. You can narrow your search a bit by knocking out all manufacturers' reps who do not also belong to ASI and SAAI. This may sound harsh, but reps who are not also members of these groups do not have access to enough products to adequately implement a program. They also are closely aligned with certain products from certain manufacturers and do not have your interests at heart. Above all, your promotional merchandise agency has to be working for you and only you. An outline of a letter you may want to use to ask for proposals is included at the end of the chapter. It will define the contenders for your account.

2. *So if I hire this agency in January and I don't buy anything until March, will I be billed for their services?*

Probably yes. The attraction for the agency to sell you merchandise at cost is that you commit to a dollar volume and that you provide consistent work. If your negotiated contract is for an hourly fee to be billed as the work is done, and there was work done, you will receive an invoice even though nothing was purchased. If your negotiated contract is for an annual amortization of estimated time against the account, you will receive an invoice every month for the same amount regardless of work performed. The upside of this arrangement for your company is that at the end of the year, you will have spent substantially less for your promotional merchandise. This must be the case or you would not have entered into the contract. You control the budget.

3. *We tried dealing with only one agency, and we were supposed to get great pricing, quantity discounts, and all that. It didn't happen. Our people in the field always came back with cheaper prices, and they were mad at us because they couldn't buy from these cheaper sources.*

If your promotional merchandise agency is selling to you at cost under the general terms of this program, this will never happen. You will never be embarrassed. Here's why. First, your people in the field will be paying the agency's cost for items. If you have a good agency, this "cost" will be less than the wholesale "cost" other agencies pay. Your agency will negotiate this additional discount with suppliers. This makes it doubly impossible that anyone in the field will come back with a better price. It is possible, however, to get a price from the field that is very close to your cost. Don't necessarily think that your agency is not selling to you at its cost. Many small businesses "in the field" when faced with agency competition from headquarters will make no profit just to irritate the national agency and try to keep the local business. These local businessmen have learned that in the past the national agencies have come and gone with some regularity. Under this program, however, nobody will have lower prices.

4. *We have a co-op program now with a catalog of ad specialties. Our ad specialty supplier inventories all our products, sells them, and invoices the buyers. We never see a bill. What could be better than that?*

A lot could be better, starting with lower prices for the catalog items. You or your buyers are paying for the storage of inventory whether the ad specialty agent tells you so or not. He or she must make sufficient profit to cover these holding costs as well as fulfillment costs. This means higher prices. You may be under the impression that the prices are lower, but when you factor in the quantities your ad specialty person is purchasing, the prices are not that low. Dollar for dollar, you are far better on an annual basis to adjust the monthly retainer to cover the extra overhead, and buy the merchandise at cost. In your co-op reimbursements alone, you will be paying substantially less since your customers will be asking for credits on the wholesale value, not the retail value of the merchandise. Additionally, customers will buy more—much more—when the price is substantially reduced, so your program will be much more successful. When this cost advantage is passed on to your customers or employees in a co-op program, the enthusiasm for quality merchandise at low prices is often enough to energize your target audience into acting on your sales message, or in the case of employees, working harder.

5. *This sounds like a lot of work. Do I really care?*
Promotional merchandise is becoming the critical element in targeted communications campaigns. Advertising and communications executives agree that the broad-brush approach to reaching audiences is ending. It is being replaced with individual messages to individuals and the groups they represent. Additionally, advertising mediums are getting more and more expensive—too expensive for many firms to use regularly to economically reach their audiences. If you don't yet care about the effect promotional merchandise can have on your business, you probably will be caring in the future simply on the basis of budget and communications trends. A head start in this area can make you a hero.

WRITING THE PROPOSAL

A centralized purchasing program proposal Clay Clay Steven & Blair submitted to a client is reprinted below. The client's name has been replaced with the fictitious name "Birdseed International."

You may copy this proposal, use it within your own company, or change it without violating any copyright laws as long as you are a merchandise buyer for a business or association. If you are an agency looking for business and you will make a profit from the use of this proposal, you can't use it. If you do, you will violate copyright laws.

CONTENTS

The proposal contains more than a simple merchandise program. In the belief that a successful program utilizes several disciplines including target audience publicity, top level management support, and ongoing review and discussion; the following program is a serious structured promotional merchandise communications program. This particular proposal has the previously mentioned cost-plus feature. The agency's profit is derived from a sliding scale markup on net sales. The agency's net overhead fee is billed each month. Although this wrinkle is a bit more complicated than a straight consulting fee, it allows headquarters management to allocate overhead costs accurately to users based on their volume. To get a rough idea of the monthly cost of a straight consulting fee, review the Savings Table, add Projected Clay Profit to Yearly Clay Overhead, and divide by 12. The savings column remains unchanged.

PROMOTIONAL MERCHANDISE CENTRALIZED PURCHASING PROPOSAL FOR BIRDSEED CORPORATION

Prepared by:
Clay Clay Steven & Blair

About This Proposal

- This proposal will explain how promotional merchandise is typically purchased, and how it may be purchased under a proposed centralized purchasing program.
- It will detail the duties of local managers as well as those of a headquarters-based group, as they relate to centralized purchasing and promotional merchandise campaign implementation.
- It will present a program of cost containment where local managers will buy products at prices well below those available in the field.
- It will detail the methods of achieving consistent quality in promotional merchandise.
- It will show how Birdseed can exercise complete control over the use of its logo, graphics and image.
- It will show how to implement this program company-wide.

Situation

1. Birdseed Corporation has offices throughout the United States which sell a variety of different brands of consumer and commercial gardening products.
2. Managers at these offices purchase—independently—promotional merchandise to complement the following types of activities:

- Sales incentive.
- Point of purchase.
- Employee motivation.
- Quality control.
- Employee anniversary.
- Company and sponsored sports teams.
- Retirement.
- Executive gifts.
- Spiffs.
- Safety awards.
- Attendance awards.
- Christmas cards and holiday gifts.
- Company stores.
- Pocket, desk, and wall calendars.

3. In addition, managers at these offices purchase—independently—other merchandise such as binders, stickers and decals, uniforms and sales wear, and name tags and name plates.
4. No hard numbers exist to determine how much is spent company-wide on merchandise of the type described in points two and three.
5. There is virtually no control over what is bought, how the Birdseed logo is used on it, or what price is paid.
6. There is no record of how many suppliers Birdseed currently uses to obtain this merchandise, or whether Birdseed is receiving the best price, quality and service for this merchandise.
7. The headquarters purchasing department has already begun a centralized purchasing program with respect to other groups of products and this centralized purchasing has been successful.

Objectives

1. To centralize the purchase of all promotional merchandise as well as merchandise not used for promotions but which carries the Birdseed or individual field or division logos.
2. To control and standardize the use of the Birdseed (and subsidiary company) logos.
3. To demonstrate a substantial dollar savings while improving quality and service standards.
4. To provide managers throughout the Birdseed network with a "management by objectives" working environment with respect to promotional merchandise.

Philosophy

The discussion of centralized versus decentralized management as related by popular business consultants, is valid in that it relies on individual managers to understand their market best and to be in a position to react most quickly to changing conditions and opportunities. This argument for decentralized management, while currently enjoying wide acceptance, is patently wasteful from a time and money standpoint when it is applied to the purchase and the efficient implementation of promotional merchandise programs.

Managers who understand their market *must* contribute to the objectives and the implementation of a promotional merchandise campaign, but giving them the responsibility of purchasing the product—or having the final word on the exact product—is asking them to utilize talents they most likely do not have.

The coordination of management talents and market knowledge available at the local level, and the addition of purchasing, programming and communications disciplines available at the headquarters level, can produce a successful promotional merchandise program.

How Merchandise Is Bought

To understand how this program will work, it is necessary to have sufficient grounding in the manufacturing and sales paths promotional merchandise follows before it reaches the local managers at Birdseed companies.

For purposes of this explanation, merchandise will be divided into two categories:

- What you could buy at a retail store.
- What you could not buy at a retail store.

Incentives, awards, door prizes, and other products make up the first group. If you give away a refrigerator, or a fishing rod and reel as an award, often the most cost effective way to purchase these products is directly from manufacturers, usually through their sales reps. Sales reps typically have a 10 percent markup on the product, they handle no billing and usually carry no inventory. When price becomes a negotiating point, the rep's commission is the first item cut. Virtually all manufacturers will cut out the rep's commission entirely in an extremely competitive situation. Sometimes the price, even without the rep's commission, is not the best price available for the product. This is especially true with electronic, photographic and household goods. Regional or national retail discounters often will carry the item at a lower cost. Additionally, manufacturers regard this market—promotional merchandise—as a dumping ground for outdated products. Manufacturers also have been known to sell merchandise to the promotion market with advertising for other products inside the packaging. They can charge other manufacturers for the right to be in the package, and offer the product at a somewhat lower price. This can have negative effects on a promotion, especially if one of the "ride along" products is a competitor.

From a centralized purchasing point of view, negotiations with key manufacturers would result in a variety of products available for such purchases at the lowest cost, highest quality, and least risk of embarrassment. Early and direct negotiations would allow manufacturers to service Birdseed as a house account, and the uncomfortable position of eliminating a rep's commission (often after that rep has actually provided a service) is nonexistent.

The second category of merchandise—what you don't buy retail—includes many items with a logo such as hats, T-shirts, pens, plaques, trophies, coffee mugs, and cheap giveaways. This industry is controlled by a for-profit corporation—Advertising Specialty Institute—in Langhorne, Pennsylvania. They have accepted the dual role of listing suppliers of this type of merchandise as well as independent businessmen who act as middlemen or agents and sell to the end users. ASI represents several thousand independent agents—most employing fewer than 10 employees with gross sales of less than $250,000 per year. At the same time it represents a few thousand manufacturers. Typically, the manufacturers provide catalogs that are price-coded and contact-blind. The agent gives these to end users with his or her business card attached, forcing the buyer to call the agent instead of the manufacturer. As with retail-type merchandise, however, large orders often find their way directly to the manufacturer and the agent is cut out of his or her profit. Unlike retail-type reps, agents—using the catalogs—can show a gross profit of 100 percent on small quantities and 60 to 80 percent on large orders. Most agents, however, discount.

Built-In Problems

With respect to both types of merchandise, there are two built-in problems which prevent good prices and good service:

- The buyer usually does not know who the manufacturer is, and therefore is unable to negotiate directly with the factory on a variety of topics such as price, delivery, returns, production technique and other details such as whether or not there is a union shop involved.
- The end user may know more about the product than the agent who is selling hundreds of products and usually does not know any single one well enough to properly represent it to the buyer.

Individual Responsibilities & Cost Containment

Under the proposed centralized purchasing program, local or headquarters managers will have the option to negotiate directly with suppliers on all subjects, including price—with the counsel of Clay Clay Steven & Blair account people. Any specific expertise or history with a certain product or market that a local manager has, can be used in the planning and negotiating stages so that programs build on each other and mistakes are not made over and over again.

From a price standpoint, under this centralized program, all products will be purchased by local managers at the wholesale price. This will eliminate the possibility of a local manager—or anyone else—obtaining a cheaper price for the same product. In addition, this "wholesale price" probably will be lower than the wholesale price paid by a smaller independent agent.

Each month, an accounting of purchases will be presented, and, based on volume, a profit margin will be assigned. Representative margins based on volume are shown on the following table under the column "Projected Clay Profit."

In addition, a direct overhead charge, billed monthly in advance, will cover personnel, capital equipment, and other direct expenses. No margin is included in this overhead charge. Birdseed and Clay jointly will determine the overhead charge using the guidelines shown in the table under the column "Yearly Clay Overhead." It will only include the actual costs of overhead incurred in carrying out the day-to-day responsibilities of the account. Auditors' statements of the authenticity of these charges will also be submitted.

The following example will compare this program with a traditional buying environment using the table below:

Current Level of Purchases per Year	*Estimated Wholesale Price*	*Clay Net %*	*Projected Clay Profit*	*Yearly Clay Overhead*	*Total Birdseed Cost*	*Total Birdseed Savings*
$ 50,000	$ 30,000	11.5	$ 3,450	$ 7,800	$ 41,250	$ 8,750
$ 60,000	$ 36,000	11.5	$ 4,140	$ 9,000	$ 49,140	$ 10,860
$ 70,000	$ 42,000	11.5	$ 4,830	$ 9,000	$ 55,830	$ 14,170
$ 80,000	$ 48,000	11.5	$ 5,520	$ 9,000	$ 62,520	$ 17,480
$ 90,000	$ 54,000	11.5	$ 6,210	$ 9,000	$ 69,210	$ 20,790
$ 100,000	$ 60,000	11.5	$ 6,900	$ 12,000	$ 78,900	$ 21,100
$ 125,000	$ 75,000	11.5	$ 8,625	$ 12,000	$ 95,625	$ 29,375
$ 150,000	$ 90,000	11.5	$ 10,350	$ 12,000	$ 112,350	$ 37,650
$ 175,000	$ 105,000	11.5	$ 12,075	$ 12,000	$ 129,075	$ 45,925
$ 200,000	$ 120,000	11.5	$ 13,800	$ 18,000	$ 151,800	$ 48,200
$ 225,000	$ 135,000	11.5	$ 15,525	$ 18,000	$ 168,525	$ 56,475
$ 250,000	$ 150,000	11.5	$ 17,250	$ 18,000	$ 185,250	$ 64,750
$ 275,000	$ 165,000	11.5	$ 18,975	$ 18,000	$ 201,975	$ 73,025
$ 300,000	$ 180,000	11.5	$ 20,700	$ 24,000	$ 224,700	$ 75,300
$ 400,000	$ 240,000	11.5	$ 27,600	$ 38,400	$ 306,000	$ 94,000
$ 500,000	$ 300,000	11.0	$ 33,000	$ 43,200	$ 376,200	$ 123,800
$ 600,000	$ 360,000	11.0	$ 39,600	$ 54,000	$ 453,600	$ 146,400
$ 700,000	$ 420,000	11.0	$ 46,200	$ 78,000	$ 544,200	$ 155,800
$ 800,000	$ 480,000	11.0	$ 52,800	$ 90,000	$ 622,800	$ 177,200
$ 900,000	$ 540,000	11.0	$ 59,400	$ 90,000	$ 689,400	$ 210,600
$1,000,000	$ 600,000	10.0	$ 60,000	$102,000	$ 762,000	$ 238,000
$1,250,000	$ 750,000	10.0	$ 75,000	$102,000	$ 927,000	$ 323,000
$1,500,000	$ 900,000	10.0	$ 90,000	$102,000	$1,092,000	$ 408,000
$1,750,000	$1,050,000	10.0	$105,000	$102,000	$1,257,000	$ 493,000
$2,000,000	$1,200,000	10.0	$120,000	$120,000	$1,440,000	$ 560,000
$2,250,000	$1,350,000	10.0	$135,000	$120,000	$1,605,000	$ 645,000
$2,500,000	$1,500,000	10.0	$150,000	$120,000	$1,770,000	$ 730,000
$2,750,000	$1,650,000	10.0	$165,000	$120,000	$1,935,000	$ 815,000
$3,000,000	$1,800,000	10.0	$180,000	$132,000	$2,112,000	$ 888,000
$3,250,000	$1,950,000	10.0	$195,000	$132,000	$2,277,000	$ 973,000
$3,500,000	$2,100,000	10.0	$210,000	$132,000	$2,442,000	$1,058,000
$3,750,000	$2,250,000	10.0	$225,000	$132,000	$2,607,000	$1,143,000
$4,000,000	$2,400,000	10.0	$240,000	$144,000	$2,784,000	$1,216,000
$4,250,000	$2,550,000	10.0	$255,000	$144,000	$2,949,000	$1,301,000
$4,500,000	$2,700,000	10.0	$270,000	$144,000	$3,114,000	$1,386,000
$4,750,000	$2,850,000	10.0	$285,000	$144,000	$3,279,000	$1,471,000
$5,000,000	$3,000,000	10.0	$300,000	$156,000	$3,456,000	$1,544,000

On purchases of $1 million per year (left column), there would be an approximate mark up of 60 percent, or a wholesale value of approximately $600,000 and a resulting profit (not shown on table)—spread among hundreds of middlemen—of $400,000.

Under the centralized purchasing program, this $600,000 worth of product at the wholesale level, would be sold directly, through one agent, to Birdseed managers. Of this, a net profit of $60,000 (10 percent of wholesale value) would be billed, along with an estimated overhead charge of $8,500 per month or $102,000 for the program year. Therefore, the total cost to Birdseed would be $762,000, compared with $1,000,000 it pays now—a $238,000 savings.

The graph below shows the savings available between $50,000 and $300,000 per year, a typical range of promotional merchandise budgets. As purchases increase, the savings become more dramatic, reaching $75,300 on expenditures of $300,000.

These dramatic dollar savings, however, are not the only tangible benefit of this centralized purchasing program.

FIGURE 8-1
Birdseed Corporation Savings Possible with Centralized Promotional Merchandise Purchasing

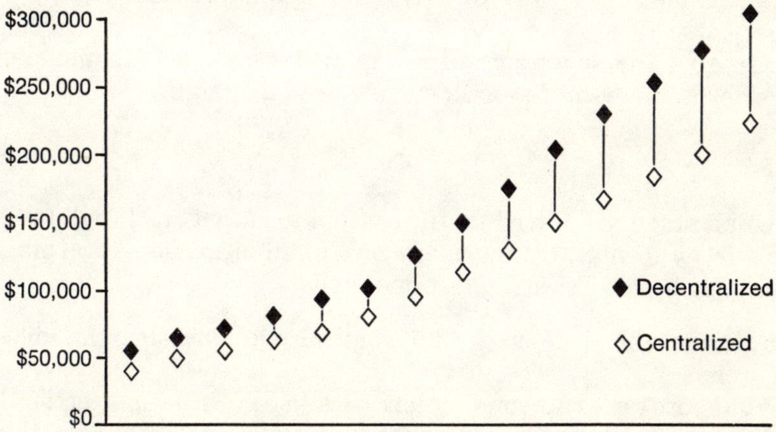

- Before purchases are made, a Clay account person and a Birdseed headquarters and field manager have reviewed the objectives of the program and confirmed that the product will do the communications job desired.
- The local manager will have the opportunity to customize his product by working directly with the manufacturer to obtain conditions most favorable to Birdseed and the individual division.
- The headquarters group will have the opportunity to make sure the product and the graphics conform to all corporate identity regulations and that the product itself furthers the image Birdseed wants its public to see.
- A continual program of case histories in newsletter format and seminars held as part existing management and marketing meetings will educate local managers, position merchandise as an integral and measurable part of the communications mix and provide the latest techniques and technology for reaching audiences.

Implementing the Program

A three-stage implementation program will achieve the following objectives:

- Audit past and anticipated purchases company-wide.
- Survey buying habits and levels of expertise in the field.
- Determine how and from whom managers are currently buying.
- Introduce the new program and gain the support of managers.
- Perform follow-up research on selected campaigns.

Stage 1

The first stage will introduce the concept to managers. It will take the survey format, asking managers for information regarding their purchases. Typical questions include:

- How far ahead do you plan your promotional merchandise purchases?
- What categories do you buy for? (See list in Situation section.)
- What are the last three purchases you made, and what were the products used for?
- What products do you plan to buy in the next 12 months, and for what purposes?

- Who do you currently buy promotional merchandise from?
- Why do you buy merchandise from this company/person?
- Do you feel you are paying too much?
- Are you satisfied with the success of your promotional merchandise program?

Stage 2

Once the answers are tabulated, the largest buyers of merchandise will be invited to a meeting at headquarters where the program will be explained in detail and their input will be solicited. During the meeting, promotional merchandise plans for the next year will be discussed, and merchandise will be researched.

Stage 3

After this meeting, the remaining managers will receive formal notice of the program along with an introductory kit which introduces the program.

There will be follow-up in case history format on the first programs, showing the effectiveness, cost savings and acceptance.

The auditing exercise where you find out your company's or division's promotional merchandise needs, as well as current buying habits, is extremely important to the acceptance and success of the program. The better the case you, as a buyer, build that supports your belief in the centralized purchase of promotional merchandise such as the one described above, the more likely you are to meet with success.

REQUEST FOR PROPOSALS

Finding agencies to submit proposals for your business can begin with a letter to those you may already know, those suggested by your advertising or public relations firm or those you chose from the Yellow Pages.

The letter should simply ask if the agency is interested in submitting a proposal based on the following criteria:

- Promotional merchandise will be sold to you at cost and the agency will be paid a negotiated fee for its time.
- Agency must submit examples of promotional merchandise programs—not individual sales—where communications objectives were attained.
- Agency must submit proof of membership in the Advertising Specialty Institute and The Specialty Advertising Association International.
- Agency must agree that if it carries exclusive or franchised lines, that it will not recommend these lines to the exclusion of competitors.
- Agency must show financial strength in accordance with your needs.
- Agency must be able to produce collateral material—newsletters, brochures and other printed material—to communicate the successes of the program and to introduce new phases. (A desktop publishing capability is a plus because you will save the expense of commercial typesetting and layout charges.)

FEW RESPONSES

Depending on who you are, you may or may not get many valid responses. If you work for a well-known company with a reputation for buying promotional merchandise, many firms will reply to your letter with an alternative plan just to get in to see you. If you would consider this a time-wasting experience and do not want to participate in it, hire an outside firm to send the letter and screen the responses. Nobody will know who you are until they get to the second round of eliminations.

TALK TO US

Once you get a list you are comfortable with—no more than three—invite each firm in to talk. Let them know what kind of program you want, and ask them to submit a proposal. If you have already performed the promotional merchandise audit, give each contender the data. If not, ask them to construct their own situation based on the information you give them at the meeting.

At the very least give them the following information:

- Current promotional merchandise budget.
- Projected promotional merchandise budget.
- Audiences.
- Communications objectives (advertising and public relations).
- Sales targets and products.
- Special problems you would like promotional merchandise to solve.
- Reporting criteria (monthly sales, meeting reports, division reports, etc.).

Decide on a date for the formal proposal and inform your management. Others may wish to attend the presentation. From this point on, the process is identical to hammering out a deal with an advertising or public relations firm. If you are not in the advertising or public relations department, you may want to ask someone who is to be your inside consultant. Negotiated points will include the profit margins, account staffing, and reporting.

HOW MUCH TO PAY?

For a single consulting arrangement, depending on what part of the country you are located, the hourly fees can range from $135 an hour for senior management in New York or California, to $35 an hour for traffickers in the southern United States. The chart below divides the country into regions and the jobs into categories with average per hour rates.

Region	*Sr. Management*	*Account Executive*	*Traffic*	*Art*
Northeast	$135.00	$95.00	$70.00	$65.00
Midwest	125.00	85.00	50.00	40.00
South	100.00	70.00	35.00	35.00
California	135.00	95.00	70.00	65.00
West	125.00	85.00	50.00	40.00

Most of your day-to-day work will be handled by traffickers with account executive time following and art time behind that. Senior management time, unless you have a need for concentrated hand-holding, should be only five hours a month, regardless of the size of your program.

FIGURING THE GOOD DEAL

Regardless of what you pay per hour, you are not going to be happy until you see the savings in the new program. To see these savings before you hire the agency you need to look at the product.

This procedure assumes that you know generally what you are going to buy and that you know how much you would pay for it ordinarily.

Give the contending agencies a list of products you will be purchasing and ask them to prepare a budget showing wholesale cost and charges for their time to service the account.

If your annual purchases are more than $50,000, the agency should save you money. If they don't, keep looking. The previous table shows ordinary wholesale costs of $50,000 in retail costs, and this chart is purposely conservative. With an agency following these guidelines, $41,250 will buy what $50,000 does under your present purchasing system. The savings go up from here.

CHAPTER 9

DOING IT YOURSELF

If you cut the lawn, you'll get grass stains on your shoes. If you don't mind the stains, if in fact you kind of like them, and if you like the smell of the cuttings and the geometry of the job—making wheel lines in the lawn—then you probably ought to be cutting your own grass.

This is the closest metaphor for wading into the purchase of promotional merchandise by yourself—especially if you plan to purchase overseas. Above all, you have to want to do it and enjoy doing it because many times, the monetary savings and the learning curve time do not justify the activity. It is easier and smarter—from one perspective—to sit at your desk and supervise the promotional merchandise buying of one or more agents. Your three-ring binders and catalogs full of products and prices can find a comfortable home on your bookshelves and in your file cabinets, while you get on with other duties.

NO GUARANTEES

While other chapters in this book deal with whether you should use an agent, whether you should purchase through a centralized program, and how to choose the right promotional merchandise, this chapter shows you how to get into the trenches and buy promotional merchandise yourself. It assumes you do not want to use an agent. This chapter carries no guarantees. If you wind up with the wrong size and color, or pay too much, or your geegaws don't show up at all; these are the risks you accept. If you find a wonderful factory owner in Brazil, Hong Kong,

Florence, or St. Louis who delivers exactly what you want at a very good price; these are the rewards you will reap.

DID YOU HOSE 'EM?

The first step to help determine whether you should buy merchandise direct is a one-question test: How great a deal did you get when you bought your last car? If you are smiling right now—that cat-that-ate-the-pigeon smile—because you drove the car dealership into Chapter 11 with your negotiating tactics, keep smiling, but don't buy your own promotional merchandise. You'll consummate the cheapest non-deals in promotional merchandise history. When you negotiate the price of promotional merchandise with a manufacturer, the merchandise often hasn't been made. This means that if you think you have made the deal of the century, you're probably wrong. The manufacturer can manufacture the goods sloppily, substitute materials, or run the order during a slow plant time—without regard for your delivery date. If you are unhappy with any of these surprise conditions, the manufacturer is often just as happy if you walk away. He hasn't much profit to lose. In contrast, once you have reached your rock bottom car price, you drive away happy. (The exception to this rule is if you are buying merchandise you can see, merchandise that can be picked up immediately and taken, and merchandise you know works and is not stolen.)

SHOULD YOU OR SHOULDN'T YOU?

Purchasing merchandise directly from a supplier requires respect for the manufacturer, courtesy, an honorable approach, and a willingness to pay a fair price. None of these attributes is necessary to get a great deal on a car.

Aside from passing the one-question test, there are guidelines for who should and should not buy direct. Who should buy direct?

- People who purchase large quantities of the same item over an extended period of time.
- People who know what they want and whose primary job is to buy promotional merchandise.

Who should not buy direct?

- Inveterate bargain hunters.
- Disinterested buyers.
- Buyers who purchase small quantities of many different items.
- Risk-avoidance practitioners.

HOW MANY IS MANY?

Before you read farther, it is important to understand the relative term *large quantities*. A large quantity of baseball caps begins at 25,000. It may, however, be prudent to buy directly and import as few as 5,000 lapel pins. A large quantity of televisions is 100. Throughout the chapter you will get a sense of the relative nature of quantity and what determines large and small quantities and their discounts. One blender at a shop that no longer carries blenders can be priced at a high quantity level (a low price).

Aside from quantities, determining when it is prudent to buy directly means identifying the type of promotional merchandise you are buying. Because, hard as you try, you will not be able to buy certain merchandise directly so don't waste your time.

WILL THEY TALK TO YOU

By now you should be familiar with the difference between an ad specialty and a premium. In the centralized purchasing chapter, promotional merchandise is broken into two categories: what you can buy in a retail store and what you can't buy in a retail store. Examples are electronics, housewares, and clothing—as opposed to combs with your logo on them or sloganed glow-in-the-dark key tags. In a very general sense, if you can buy it retail, it's a premium. If you can't, it's an ad specialty. Don't argue with me about this. The distinction works well in this chapter.

The key is whether the manufacturers of these items will sell them to you—the personnel manager or the safety director or the middlest of middle managers at the most homogeneous corporation in America—without a middleman's profit slipped in. There is also the matter of finding these suppliers.

CALL THEM

Retail promotional merchandise like housewares and electronics or fitness machines or any sexy, trendy items you see in the sexy trendy mail order catalogs, is bought—or not bought—at wholesale. It depends on how good a negotiator you are. Start by calling the company directly. It is not necessary to tell them you are purchasing these goods for a premium, incentive, award, contest, sweepstakes, or any other label that will deliver you directly to the premium sales department. If you wind up here—and you are intent on buying direct—you have lost. Ninety-nine percent of the time the area rep's commission (5 to 10 percent) is in your price. The reps are making money from your sale, and they will not lift a pencil or hit a key on a computer to earn it. So if you are serious about buying direct, do not go to the premium sales department.

SCUFFLING ONWARD

Many buyers who get into scuffles with their premium reps, call the company directly and announce their intentions to—from this minute onward—deal directly with the factory, or not deal at all. The factory is more than happy to continue selling to this customer, leading him or her to believe that the rep is out of the loop when, in reality, the rep still receives a commission on every order placed directly with the factory.

But there is another reason for avoiding the premium sales department besides not wanting to pay a rep's commission. This department's prices are consistently higher than what you would pay for the same item at a retail discounter. Yes, the premium "wholesale" price is most often higher than what you would pay if you put on your old pants and tennis shoes and offered up your Visa card at the nearest discount store. This is especially true with electronics, computers, housewares, and cameras. The simple fact is that premium buyers are not as good at negotiating prices as are retail store buyers. There are several reasons for this, including the quantity bought and the quality of the ongoing relationship that retail buyers have and that premium buyers usually do not care to establish.

CAN'T GET IT FROM HERE

The price disparity is not simply a matter of marking up the same model a notch or two before it is shipped to a premium buyer. Many manufacturers regularly produce models for retail distribution only, or for discount retail distribution only. So the television you see—whether it's a Sony or something else—at your local discount electronics house, may very well not even be available from your premium rep or through the premium sales department, let alone available at a great price. These models are produced to satisfy the demand of large discount retailers who want to offer a prestigious name at a very low price.

WORSE THAN RETAIL

If you need graphic proof of the price disparity, go to a local discount electronics store, find a bargain name-brand television and call your premium rep to get a comparable price. If your rep carries this model—which is doubtful—it will be more expensive. Period. It is probable that your rep will explain that this is a model that is being phased out, or it was a low production run model, or it is a model that has already been replaced, or—the truth—that the model simply isn't available to the premium market. You know, as does even the greenest buyer, that the last serious improvements to televisions were the transistor and the remote control. This year's model has "knob difference" if that, when compared to last year's so why should you pay more for a new knob?

If you want to try to avoid this premium on premiums, deal with the retail sales department. Tell them what you want to buy, how many, what model number, what color, and where you will pick them up. Of course, you will know all this before you make the call. You will have found the information from scouring retail stores—not from reading premium trade magazines. The model numbers, the names of the products, and the phone numbers given in these trade publications zap you right into the premium sales department.

ARE YOU A GOOD CUSTOMER?

If you can get through to the retail sales department—not the premium sales department—you will only interest these people if you are what they consider to be a good customer. Being a good customer might include your willingness to purchase a model that is not moving so well, or to take delivery right away, or to pay right away, or to pick up items yourself, or to buy what the seller considers to be a large quantity. In one case, a manufacturer agreed to contact a distributor who had a large inventory of glasses, and the distributor sold them directly to the buyer at a low price the manufacturer dictated. The distributor knew that if he didn't sell this inventory, he couldn't finance a new order or have any place to store it. The manufacturer knew this too and wanted to sell the new order. The deal was made with the help of a willing buyer who took the time to understand the motivating factors governing the sale. Good agents uncover these situations all the time. You will too, if you are a good buyer.

RESELLING OUT

Often a seller is concerned about resale on a direct sale. If the seller wants to know what you are going to do with the product, he probably really wants to know what you're not going to do with it. When asked this question, avoid being zipped into the premium sales department by saying you are not going to resell it, but you are going to use it within your company. If you use the word "premium," "incentive," or any of the other key words, the person in the sales department may feel that he or she must follow company policy and give you to the premium sales department.

If the person at the other end of the phone absolutely says you must deal with the premium sales department, and you say you would rather not, you can justify your response with the following:

- Premium department prices are generally higher.
- Your company is willing to forego the service offered by a premium rep. You know exactly what you want and what price you would like to pay.
- Your company has a policy of buying directly, and you have not previously contacted a premium rep who handles this line.

STRATEGY TWO

Sometimes, however, a premium manufacturer just will not deal with you. When this happens, ask who his biggest distributor is. If there aren't distributors, ask who the biggest retailer of his products is. Go see this person. You will have a deal if you want one. This is especially true in housewares and electronics—two of the most popular premium item categories.

Arrange to meet with someone who has the power to negotiate. Make an appointment and then do your homework. Remember, this guy is not the biggest retailer or distributor because he is a pushover. He's very likely looking at you as a fat-in-the-wallet corporate buyer who is looking for a few hair dryers and TVs and doesn't know what to pay for them. He may interpret his job as one of salesman extraordinaire and attempt to sell you products that will provide him with the highest markup, not products advertised as specials designed to get customers into the store. If this describes you, save yourself the trip and call your premium rep. You could get better service at the same high price sitting in your office with the rep drinking coffee and looking through a loose-leaf binder.

If this isn't you, it is paramount that you listen and remain flexible when you meet with the distributor or retailer. If you have your heart set on a model 12SPX and the distributor has a truckload of 12PPX's, find out what the difference is and negotiate. The pickier you get, the higher your price.

BUY NOW, NOT LATER

A retailer or a distributor wants to move goods and be paid for them as quickly as possible. Don't go shopping six months out with a purchase order. Buy what you need—especially in electronics, housewares, and jewelry—when you need it. And bring a check or negotiate COD terms if you think the seller won't deliver what he promises. Nobody in this line of work is interested in what you need six months from now, or what samples you would like, or how good your company's credit is. These are the concerns of premium reps.

Delivery is an important negotiating point. This retailer may not have a commercial carrier or delivery service that he is willing to offer at the price you are discussing. Negotiate delivery separately against what your own company trucks might be able to provide, or what a commercial carrier would handle. Don't let your profits get sucked up in delivery charges, but also don't wind up loading merchandise into your brother-in-law's van one rainy Wednesday night just to save a few dollars. When the VCRs fall out of the van, you just won—the hard way—this year's incentive awards. Make sure you specify inside or curb delivery. The terms mean exactly what you think they mean. The seller is always negotiating curb delivery, and an unwary buyer is negotiating inside delivery. It's too late when the coffee makers and vacuum cleaners are waiting for you on the corner. If you want items drop shipped, and you can't do it in-house, you could be shocked to learn how expensive it is. Factor this into your overall costs. Sometimes it is cheaper to go back to the premium rep who has drop-ship capability (usually through the premium sales department of the manufacturer).

If there is installation or assembly necessary (computers, big screen TVs, washers, dryers, and other like items) negotiate who is going to do it. Again, the seller doesn't want to. It'll cost if he does.

GRAY MARKET CAN BE PREMIUM

Negotiate return and warranty policies, and while you are doing this, determine whether the merchandise is American or gray market.

Gray market, for anyone who has been dealing strictly with manufacturer's reps since the mid-70's, is merchandise originally intended for sale to a market outside the United States. As this book goes to press in late 1988, the practice is waning. Many companies, especially German and Far East companies, know their products command a higher price in the United States, so they take advantage of this market condition and raise the price. Gray market autos have been skated to the United States from Germany, Italy, and France by entrepreneurs who buy them there and ship them over. Even within the United States a quasi-gray market can exist when a distributor buys large quantities of products and then resells them to smaller distributors and retailers around the country cheaper than they could purchase directly from the manufacturer. A well-known copier company fell into this trap a few years ago, realizing it soon after the celebration marking its single biggest sale. The company's small dealers bought from the large distributor for nearly six months. You, as a buyer, can take advantage of this situation if you know about it. Again, agents know about these goings-on, as well as who the distributors are who bought too much and are in trouble.

FAR EAST GRAY

Cameras and electronics are another shade of gray. Often, as a buyer dealing with a large distributor, you won't know whether the goods are gray or not. One way you can tell is to look at the literature packed inside the boxes. If it's not in American

English (as opposed to English English), it's probably gray. If it's in three or four languages, including American English, it's usually OK. It's not illegal to buy gray market products, but be careful about warranty work. It's probably not worth the trouble to send your camera back to Tokyo when the shutter won't shut. You'll have to decide whether warranty work is an important issue. Some things just don't break. If they work when you take them out of the box, they work. Calculators, can openers, blenders, and humidifiers fall into this category. So if you are buying a reputable gray brand, and you can live with a couple of them that don't work, the risk may be worth taking.

DOLLAR DEALS UNITED STATES A GRAY HAND

Gray markets also exist because of the fluctuation of the dollar against other currencies. Again, you need to be ready to buy, because six months out, the gray market deal probably won't be there. It is obvious that U.S. companies selling goods manufactured overseas do not like gray market goods. It lowers their sales and profits, and causes headaches and bad customer relations when unknowing consumers—maybe your award winners—bring gray products in for service. Be careful of the long-term negative effects of buying gray market goods, including the effect it may have on your reputation and your company's ability to sell goods. If, for example, your company is selling cleaning supplies to Panasonic, you might consider the bad will that could be generated when Panasonic finds out you just purchased several thousand dollars worth of gray market stereos. You could find yourself without a customer.

CAN'T GET IT RETAIL

What about the promotional merchandise that isn't sold retail? The items like key tags, T-shirts, hats, coffee mugs, and plaques are usually sold through a single-stage distribution system within an umbrella corporation called Advertising Specialty

Institute (ASI). Manufacturers of imprinted items all over North America can belong to ASI, providing they meet minimum financial and sales standards. Independent business people who want to act as agents or middlemen between the manufacturers and the buyers are called distributors, and they too can belong to ASI after passing certain minimum financial and sales criteria. Advertising, public relations, sales promotion, and marketing consulting firms also can join ASI, and be able to buy these kinds of items wholesale, but most don't realize it.

ASI, nestled in Langhorne, Pennsylvania, is the great facilitator in the geegaw world. Its substantial publications listing distributors and manufacturers and products and prices and delivery dates and credit reports are circulated among members. These publications—including the house organs and newsletters—are guarded items which each member promises to keep confidential. If you, a buyer, got your hands on this information, you could know in a few minutes where to buy those pens that look like nails, or those tape measures in the shape of houses, or those little plastic do-hickeys that pop open beer and soda cans. Many member manufacturers restrict their sales efforts to ASI listed distributors. Others choose only to deal with selected ASI distributors. Still others will deal with whomever shows up first with the order—buyers or ASI distributors.

CATALOGS WITH NO NAMES

You, as a buyer, are probably being ASI'd if you're buying geegaws and giveaways. The easiest way to tell is to look at a catalog a middleman has left. If it has a five-digit number somewhere on the front cover, possibly preceded with the letters ASI, that manufacturer belongs to ASI. These catalogs have coded prices that already are marked up so a distributor can make a profit, and they are usually complete with ordering and production information. One thing ASI catalogs don't have is the name and address of the manufacturer. The distributor knows this through the number on the cover.

BIG DEAL

As a buyer, this information about ASI is of little use. Those manufacturers who want to deal directly with you will advertise in the premium, motivation, and sales incentive publications, or in the Yellow Pages. (While premium ads in the incentive magazines will connect you with a middleman, geegaw ads usually put you directly to the manufacturers, but be alert for agents.) You can also check the *Thomas Register,* although sometimes this can get arcane. The manufacturers who don't want to deal with you will say no even if you found a way to contact them. The phrase "say no" can take on a subtle meaning in some cases. In one instance, a well-known amusement park in the Midwest found the name of the manufacturer supplying several items and demanded to deal directly. After threatening to go to another supplier, the current one offered to deal directly with the amusement park and gave the park a discount, but kept a small percent for the distributor who originally placed the order. The amusement park has no idea that the distributor, whom they refused to work with, is doing nothing for them and making a commission.

THREE SIDES OF THE ISSUE

Whether this practice is right or wrong is your decision. Viewed from one side, the distributor most likely was an unnecessary part of the transaction as it became repetitious. As the dollars got bigger, this unnecessary involvement became noticeable. The buyer became experienced enough to purchase the goods without benefit of an agent. From the manufacturer's view, the buyer was definitely a more credit-worthy customer, and the buyer might just as easily have gone somewhere else. Viewed from the disinterested observer's side, is it right to let a customer believe there is a direct deal when in fact there isn't? Someone is still getting a commission. Or, is it any business of the buyer's what the manufacturer does with its money? Should the distributor have proven his worth before the buyer got to the point where he wanted to deal direct? Should the distributor have been a little less greedy and given the buyer a better price?

FAIR-WEATHER ETHICS

Buyers who search for the cheap price after learning how to get it at the feet of distributors and reps irritate the middlemen the most. These fair-weather ethics implemented by those who profess to value their middlemen until the company MBA offers a profit-contingent bonus plan, are partly responsible for the tarnished image of the industry. Many buyers have reconciled what they consider to be a responsibility to a distributor against a responsibility to search for the company-mandated cheapest price by using distributors only if they have to. They will not call a distributor unless they have searched available outlets for the product they want. This search, incidentally, often includes the New York City Yellow Pages. At the time this book is written, there are two versions. One is published by NYNEX, called the *NYNEX Yellow Pages,* and the other is *The New York Yellow Pages* published by Southwestern Bell. Both are invaluable if you are looking for suppliers. Not oblivious to the corporate uses of these books, distributors and manufacturer's reps have listed themselves slyly in an effort to lead you to believe they are the source when in fact they are an intermediary.

TRADE SHOWS HOLD TRADE SECRETS

There are two industry trade shows, which, even if you are a casual buyer, you should attend. They are the New York Premium & Incentive Show at the Jacob Javits Center and the Chicago Premium Show at McCormick Place. They are managed by Thalheim International in Mt. Vernon, New York. These shows have everything from washers and dryers to drink stirrers. Some of the merchandise is premiums, some ad specialties, some imported, and some from ASI suppliers who deal directly. There also is the National Sporting Goods Show, The National

Stationery Show, and the Merchandise Show, all in New York. Though they are geared to retail sales outlets, a creative buyer can find trendy items at these shows and buy them directly from the manufacturer.

The premium shows—New York and Chicago—are 80 percent look and 20 percent buy. The stationery, sporting goods and merchandise shows are 80 percent buy. So, at the buying shows, be ready to confront eager salespeople with pen and clipboard. If you see something you like at these shows, offer to buy it off the floor when the show is over. Most companies don't like to ship the goods back and will sell the display items. If you want the best price, offer cash because these sales often don't make it into the company revenue figures.

BUT SERIOUSLY, BUYERS . . .

Going to these shows, however, will not make you an expert. If you are a serious direct buyer, you should be selling your subordinates to get into the Specialty Advertising Association International fete in Dallas. Getting in, however, probably isn't going to happen for you. The odds of getting a date with Olivia Newton John or Harrison Ford (choice is up to you) are better than getting a badge for this show. It is open only to SAAI members or ASI listed distributors and suppliers—they don't even like the press much. Besides the Dallas show, there are regional shows going on all the time, most of these, however, are open only to ASI and SAAI members. An ASI-listed distributor or SAAI member in your area can tell you which regional shows are open. But, if you begin a relationship with a distributor when your intention is to buy direct, you have to draw the line between deception and the best price.

THEY HEAR YOU KNOCKING, BUT . . .

From a philosophical perspective, there is an unnecessary restriction of information under the present SAAI trade show rules. These restrictions exist because of the penny-pinching ways of promotional merchandise buyers. The result is that the very people—buyers—who should be exposed to this merchandise and these suppliers, are the ones who aren't allowed through the doors. If they were, buyers could put up to 7,000 middlemen out of business the same way Congress could put a couple million accountants (and IRS agents) out of business by passing the often-proposed three-line tax return.

It is the manufacturers who have made the decision not to employ a full-time sales force, but to use distributors; however, it is the buyers who often blindly search for the cheapest price at the expense of the best doodad and the best service. Under the present system, buyers are kept away from the products and ideas that could make their programs a success because they can't be trusted to look at the best collection of merchandise without trying to buy it directly. That it is the distributor's job to bring news of new products and new ideas to buyers is nonsense. No distributor can know enough about what is going on inside a company—or what a buyer personally likes—to decide what to pitch and what to pitch out. In addition, distributor motivations often are not pure. Contest, sales incentives, and rebates often prompt a distributor to promote one product over another. The buyer never knows.

LIKELY TARGETS

So where do you start in your efforts to buy ad specialties directly, in light of what you already know? Start with the easily accessible manufacturers who make the most competitive and popular products.

- Plaques, trophies.
- T-shirts, jackets, hats, golf shirts, sweaters.
- Lucite embedments.
- Banners, flags.
- Imprinted electronics such as calculators, clocks, watches, cassette players.

Undoubtedly, the biggest category is wearables, and in this category is the ubiquitous T-shirt. It is a good item to buy direct because there are so many suppliers who are willing to sell to you.

John Caruso is half owner of St. Louis Sportswear. He is the kind of person who looks at the little gold eye in the St. Louis Cardinals logo that blankets the city on merchandise and notices whether it overlaps the outline. “Some older automatic machines do not do a good job,” he says referring to the cardinal's crossed eye. “A better screen print across the board is a hand print. A machine can get out of whack in the middle of a run.”

He and Tim James—the other half of St. Louis Sportswear—were chosen for this chapter for the following reasons:

• They have been in business 12 years—a long life in the imprinted T-shirt business. (According to *Impressions* Magazine, an industry trade publication, 67 percent of silk-screen businesses fail.)
• They deal with distributors, reps, directly with end users, and sometimes with the retail market.
• They have a clear policy about selling, and they stick to it.
• They handle sportswear silk screening (including golf shirts, jackets, T-shirts, team uniforms, beach towels, tote bags) out of their St. Louis plant, in quantities under 5,000. (They do not use automatic printing machines, so above 5,000 pieces they are not usually competitive.)
• They will purchase the wearable for you and print it, or they will print on your merchandise.
• They will accept small orders.
• They have high quality standards, and they solve problems with an attitude that keeps customers happy.
• They are not members of ASI or SAAI. This means they cannot be accused of violating association rules by giving away what might be considered confidential information. They do not have a catalog—coded or otherwise.
• John or Tim usually answers the phone so customers deal directly with management, “not a clerk who has been versed for two hours on how to handle a screen printing call.”

WHO'S YOUR FAVORITE?

Although their business is split about evenly between middlemen and end users, they prefer middlemen. If you can emulate the middleman when dealing directly, you can get better service, and better results.

"Generally the middlemen give bigger orders. They have done the leg work. They know the answers to the questions. They are calling with an order," Mr. Caruso says.

"With the consumer [direct buyer], I have to do the leg work. This means I have to explain sizing, pricing, packaging, colors, and screen printing," he adds.

Each of these topics can take a long time to explain. "Most laymen," he says, "do not know how to buy sizes. Women's sizing is the biggest problem, children's is second. For our type of imprinted sportswear, sizing is usually men's small, medium, large, extra large and extra extra large. Most people know what sizes these are. But, depending on the manufacturer—especially with jackets—a large from one company could be a small from another. It depends on the style of the jacket, too," he says. "If it has raglan sleeves, it is smaller and has a smaller imprint area."

BIGGER USUALLY BETTER

Mr. Caruso's advice to buyers who do not know what size they really need is to buy the bigger size "if it is a windbreaker, a $20 item. They are not Bill Blass suits. If there is enough time, if they are expensive, and you are picky, ask for samples," he adds. "You can get actual sleeve length and finished dimensions from any reputable manufacturer, and you can go from there. But," he cautions, "don't squeeze your printer into a deadline [he can't meet] while you are looking at samples."

"A custom jacket," he says, "with unique color combinations, special sizing and special graphics, can be really neat, but you need time to come up with the right product."

START THE PRESSES

Good printing is as much the responsibility of the buyer as the screen printer.

"Buyers have to thoroughly understand what they are asking me to imprint," Mr. Caruso says.

"We don't do transfers here [a photo process where a plastic skin is ironed on], just silk screening. The easiest job to print is a one-color imprint on a jersey knit [T-shirt weave]. The flatter the surface and the darker the lines, the better the imprint," he says. "If you want lots of detail, several colors and close registration [different colors right next to each other] on a non-flat surface like a sweater or a rib-knit, it is more complicated.

"If you're not sure of what the finished product will look like, ask for a sample," Mr. Caruso says, quickly adding that, "on my end it's the biggest pain in the neck in the world when we have to print one item, especially if you have been dealing with me and I haven't let you down before. Most of the time," he says, "you could look at a stat and save the money [used to produce a sample]."

There are times a sample is absolutely necessary, Mr. Caruso says: "When I question whether the imprint will work because of the material or the design, you should ask for a spec [sample]."

One instance was when St. Louis Sportswear was asked to print on lycra bathing suits: "We did a spec sample, and when it went through the dryers [325 degrees], it came out the size of a penny."

SCREEN PRINTING SUBTLETIES SEPARATE SEASONED FROM STARTERS

To a buyer who is not familiar with the subtleties of screen printing, normal processes could be a surprise.

Mr. Caruso explains, "The athletic market uses a heavy-weight football jersey, for example. A football coach wants a nice thick bold imprint that can take abuse. A visibly thick imprint, to him, looks great. The more ink that is piled on, the more he likes it," he says.

"On the other hand, a guy who orders golf shirts wants his imprint to have a dye effect—no ink build-up at all on his three-color imprint on an interlock fabric golf shirt. If you put a big thick print on it, it looks tacky. Sportswear has a smaller imprint, athletic wear is bigger. If it is a high school, they want it big, but if it is MAN B&W Diesel [a company that makes ship engines], they don't want to read it three holes away," he says, referring to a golf shirt worn on the links.

"Occasionally," Mr. Caruso says, "we will recommend how large an imprint should be, but we really want the buyer to tell us."

WHAT'S GOOD?

Just as some direct buyers don't know the exact size of the imprint, or even how large or small it is possible to print, many don't know what to expect from the finished product. What's good and what's unacceptable, and what do you do when you have goods you think are bad?

"Every Tuesday night at bowling," Mr. Caruso says, "I see evidence of amateur screen printers. They print white on a maroon shirt and the print comes out pink. If you can tell what kind of mesh they used," he continues, "there is an amateur." Mesh refers to the screen holes used in printing. There are several sizes for varying jobs. Your print should never look like a screen from a screen door was used. "It's those little squares that give it away," Mr. Caruso says.

He continues: "The top of the letter has a heavy build up and the bottom is fading because of a bad application, the straightness on the garment, the location, where do you put a pattern, how far can you go?"

"Softball jerseys," he says interrupting himself, "are classic examples. If the imprint is within three inches of the bottom of the shirt and the guy has a beer gut, it looks horrible. And if the imprint is low and you tuck the shirt in, the imprint is cut off."

In the laundry list of what to look for in wearables screening, Mr. Caruso also talks about "adherence to the garment. Is the imprint cracking, peeling or chipping? If it is, the ink was not cured at the right temperature. If it is coming off a jacket, it is the wrong type of ink. Not enough catalyst. Jackets aren't easy to print," he concludes.

BUT HOW MUCH IS IT?

Survey after survey has shown that price is what most interests buyers, and what motivates them to use one supplier over another.

"If a caller insists on pricing right away, I give it to him," Mr. Caruso says. "But I figure he is shopping around town and probably isn't comparing apples to apples.

"I quoted you," he says to an imaginary customer, "a Hanes white T-shirt. I have been in business for 12 years. We will replace the shirt if it is bad. My price is a finished price—no screen or hidden charges. I can give you a list of happy customers.

"If a buyer buys on price—I've seen a dime per shirt swing a 700-piece order—he is a fool. We are a bit higher on T-shirts and very competitive on other sportswear," Mr. Caruso admits, "but if a buyer uses price alone, there is an 80 percent chance of getting an inferior garment or print. For a dime, he is giving up on-time delivery, ink that stays on, a sharp, clear print, and the sizes and colors he wants."

But what about buying a cheap shirt? Does everyone need a Hanes-quality garment? Mr. Caruso, who says he has never purchased a cheap cotton shirt like the ones made in Pakistan, says, "a cheap Pakistani shirt with a terrible screen is never acceptable. There is a place for a Pakistani T-shirt with an adequate imprint. Maybe for a benefit marathon where it will only be worn once. If a customer came to me and said he wanted the cheapest shirt he could get for a pie-throwing contest, I would get it, but it would have a good imprint."

FINDING THE RIGHT SCREENER

The Yellow Pages, Mr. Caruso says, is the first place to start if you are looking for silk-screener. Where to look in the yellow book, is another question, however. "There are [categories for] garments, screen printing, imprinted sportswear, and sporting goods. We didn't want to go under sporting goods," Mr. Caruso says, "because we didn't want to specialize in team uniforms; we want corporate business. About the best place to look is under screen printing," he says. "That's where we are listed."

If you are serious about establishing a relationship with a screen printer, Mr. Caruso says, do the following:

- Ask for samples of work similar to the type of work you want done. If you want to buy screen printed golf shirts or jackets, ask for them.
- Ask for references and call them.
- Visit the factory, but don't expect it to be in a high-rent district. "Our factory is in a terrible neighborhood, but that keeps our overhead low," Mr. Caruso says. (One reason to go to the factory is to see if there really is a factory, or if you are dealing with an intermediary.)

SO WHERE ARE THE SAVINGS?

On a first order, Mr. Caruso will not usually give a direct buyer the same price he would given an established middleman. However, once the middleman adds markup, the price Mr. Caruso gives a corporate buyer could be less. Serious pricing for direct buyers is contingent on the amount of middleman's work St. Louis Sportswear must do and the amount of business they can expect. It is after the establishment of this relationship—based on repeat business and knowledge of the industry—that buyers can enjoy substantial savings while preserving quality materials and workmanship. The manufacturer's profit is never disturbed.

LABOR, MATERIALS, AND SELLING COSTS

Often when a buyer looks for ways to cut corners, he or she often cuts material quality, workmanship, or service. It isn't necessary to lose these when you want to reduce prices, if you know where to reduce. There are three components in a basic ad specialty job—whether it's T-shirts or key tags:

- Labor.
- Materials.
- Selling costs.

Intelligent price reductions, demand examination of these.

Labor is more expensive in the United States than in the Far East. If your item is labor intensive and if you meet other qualifications such as quantity and production time, the most dramatic way to reduce the cost of your promotional merchandise is to stop sending your purchase orders to Minnesota and start sending letters of credit to Mainland China.

Materials, the second cost in an item, should also be examined geographically. Plastics and ceramics are often cheaper in the Far East. Quality printing can be cheaper in Japan, Germany, and Italy. Leather is cheap in Brazil. Again, if your situation warrants it, examine the possibility of purchasing raw materials in one country and manufacturing in another. Selling costs make up the third component in this model. These can be reduced greatly, if you are willing to do the leg work Mr. Caruso talks about with every product you buy. Often, manufacturers who refuse to sell direct do so because corporate and association buyers are such demanding buffoons. They gladly turn over this black comedy of a job to a distributor. To work directly with a manufacturer and receive consistently good pricing, you—the buyer—have to learn how to serve the manufacturer. The word *serve* is used with all its demanding connotation, because in order to get a good price, you have to save the manufacturer time, aggravation, and mistakes.

ALFA INTERNATIONAL EXPERIENCED IMPORTER

The concepts related above about labor, materials, and selling costs are ideas of Mr. Greg Carrino, president of Alfa International Corp., an importing firm with a foothold in the promotional merchandise business. As with St. Louis Sportswear, Alfa International is not a member of ASI or SAAI. As the sublicensee of Adidas, theirs was the official jacket of the United States Olympic Committee 1988 Seoul Olympics. This $8 million (fiscal 1989 projection) NASDAQ-listed company (symbol ALFE) also produced the Michael Jackson "Bad" jacket as well as lesser known—but nonetheless important to their buyers—jackets for corporations and associations.

What distinguishes Alfa from other firms is:

- The material its jackets are made from: Tyvek(TM). Tyvek(TM) is a DuPont material initially developed for industry. It is used to wrap new construction housing for insulation as well as for envelopes that won't tear. It is very lightweight—the Olympic jacket weighed four ounces—and it is very warm. It is, according to Mr. Carrino, "the best windbreaker you can wear. It is sufficiently waterproof that if you get caught in the rain, you won't get wet. It is a relatively new material to the jacket industry."
- Alfa's imprinting process. "We developed specialty inks and a few pieces of specialty equipment that we adapted to our presses, and we came up with a quality equal to a photograph. We sell graphics," he says, "not jackets. We try to do the impossible, reproduce photos."
- Alfa International looks at the world as its source of materials and labor. U.S.-made Tyvek(TM) is exported to Milano, Italy, where the jackets are cut, assembled, and printed, because, as Mr. Carrino says, "In Italy, everything is art whether you like it or not. As you walk through the streets you soak in it. They have developed printing that is incredible. Their glossy printing for

art books is far superior to what is available in this country, in my opinion," he adds.

• Mr. Carrino has learned international trade from the docks up. When he was 16, he would jump on the number 35 bus out of Hackensack, New Jersey, at 3 A.M. so he could sign up on a ship bound for South America at 5:30. He worked at the Port of New York with the National Maritime Union, and speaks Italian, Spanish, and English. In addition to its jacket business, Alfa International does business in the Far East, importing video cassettes and loud speaker components.

DETAIL, DETAIL, DETAIL

Mr. Carrino, interviewed specifically for his views on how buyers could purchase promotional merchandise directly from overseas manufacturers, would not stop referring to details. "You cannot take anything for granted," he says. "You cannot do it by fax, mail and telex. It is very important to establish a personal relationship with your trading partner. Do it right the first time," he says. "No one can teach you. You have to learn by dealing. Americans in business tend to be very lax in the way we go about things. We don't pay attention to detail. If there is one thing that will kill you, it is lack of attention to detail.

"If you send camera-ready art overseas and it is not perfect," he says, "it will be reproduced that way. You must be very specific. You can't assume that people automatically know your customs—that toothpaste always comes in the same kind of tube because it doesn't. The size of envelopes is different, so if you are printing something to go into an envelope, you have to know European sizes from U.S. sizes. I routinely give all measurements in metric and inches.

FELL OFF THE BACK OF A SHIP

"But," he adds, "things still go wrong. Containers fall off ships, U.S. Customs holds shipments, somebody is trying to smuggle drugs on the ship your cargo is on, people steal things. There are endless numbers of problems, but the more you do it, the better you get, providing you like what you are doing and can learn from your mistakes," he says.

Things can go wrong or right, depending on how the deal is negotiated. Although Mr. Carrino feels he is an equal negotiator to any of his suppliers or his competition, he says, "we are perhaps the worst negotiators in the world," speaking of U.S. citizens.

"When we negotiate," he adds, "we send our top guy and the other side sends a middle manager. Once that session is over, our top guy meets with the other side's upper middle manager. Then, our top guy meets with the boss and they clean your clock every time. Three times they have picked up negotiations where the last man left off, and each time, we thought we were through negotiating," he says.

"Many American middle managers don't understand that the middle manager they are negotiating with in Europe or in the Far East is going to do the best job he can at his level. He is proud to be working for his company. Middle management here," he adds, "isn't usually too prepared. They don't have the same attitude."

Mr. Carrino says he would go overseas (Far East) for 25,000 caps. "There is no quota on caps there," he says. "We contract and manufacture Tyvek™ hats there. We did our homework and found a good manufacturer. Certainly," he says of high quantities, "50,000 of anything is a lot, but not to the guy who is making them on a day-by-day basis. Your problem is controlling quality. Once they cash your letter of credit and they have spelled your name wrong [on the hats] , you better know how to handle the situation.

"The guy who was brought up in the suburbs and who has never been overseas should use an agent," Mr. Carrino says. "He will still save money if the quantities are sufficient. If the guy [referring to a buyer] is from the streets, is able to adapt to situations, and knows what to do in the worst situations, he probably will be okay."

"He [the buyer] will have to understand that in the Far East, people from one factory will try to keep him isolated. He will have to say 'I want to see factory B.' And, they will say, 'no, no, stay with us.' "

An agent, however, can save a lot of aggravation and still save a buyer money. "The agent knows that if he does a good job, there is a possibility that he will work again. People overseas make a lower hourly rate, so for them to make 5 or 10 percent commission is a lot of money," Mr. Carrino says. "Even though," he adds, "it may not be a lot to you. His culture, his instinct, is going to tell him to do a good job."

Mr. Carrino reflects for a moment and says, "we have ruined a lot of companies over there. We have cheated a lot of people, and there are a lot of agents just waiting to take your money. A buyer has to be willing to take a flight over to meet the people and to judge."

As for price, Mr. Carrino says, "I wouldn't try to beat the guy up. Although," he says, "it gets to be an ego thing with a lot of people." The buyer says 'I work for [company name omitted] and I can make your company, so I want a cheap price.' "

Mr. Carrino says this is not his way of negotiating the best deal.

A relationship depends on "volume, repeat business, the time frame. If it's a spot buy, it's not worth the time and trouble to do it yourself, and if it's for the long-term, you have to create a good relationship." For example, Mr. Carrino never asks for free samples. "We want nothing for nothing," he says. "We want to treat our suppliers with the respect that we would like to be treated with. I am willing to make an investment by paying for the samples, freight and duty. I don't ask a factory to make an investment in our market. Don't take me to lunch or dinner, or give me theater tickets. Give me service, not lip service. If you tell me you are going to put the box on the water [container on a ship], put it on the water."

CHAPTER 10

APPRECIATING THE SUBTLETIES

There was a time when you did not have to turn down the volume during a TV commercial. The sound levels of the sitcom—even with the laugh track—and the Toyota Sale-athon ("Deals, Deals, Deals") were relatively equal. Then, with an ear to the short-term attention span of many TV viewers, advertisers and their agencies realized that yelling at you tends to get your attention, and a new derivation of noise pollution was born.

It was only a derivation, however. Promotional merchandise is the originator of obnoxious message conveyance—a pollutant long before PCB's, chloroflurocarbons, or screaming TV commercials.

Unfortunately a television commercial that does not scream at you stands a good chance of going unnoticed. (At the very least, you won't hear it from the kitchen or the bathroom.)

Fortunately, promotional merchandise does not need to be overbearing to get your attention. Subtle promotional merchandise can also be powerful promotional merchandise. The medium is not restricted—as traditional advertising is—by column inches, video tape, the size of the bus ad, or the decibel level of the audio. The restrictions in promotional merchandise lie in its misuse, not its physical limitations.

If this book has done anything, it should have brought you to the point where you are the purchaser of powerful promotional merchandise. The product and the message do your talking for you, and when the two are saying the same thing in a cost-efficient manner, you have successful promotional merchandise communication. Now, in the last few pages, words about being subtle.

If television commercials and doodads can be compared, the volume on a commercial is analogous to the message on promotional merchandise. If the design—the logo, the slogan, or the art—yells at you like a 2 A.M. 30-second spot for aluminum windows, it won't matter how good the merchandise itself is, the message is apt to be dismissed.

SUBTLE AND COMMON

Even the most common geegaw like a button or a bumper sticker, when it carries the right message, is powerful persuasion. Barry Goldwater's 1960 campaign produced the message: *AU* H_2O, the letter designators for gold and water from the Periodic Table of the Elements. Granted, it was not enough to overcome voters' perception that he would wage nuclear war with the Russians, but the medium—the button and the bumper sticker—was well served with this creative message. In 1952, Harriman's portable fan, given out to sweltering delegates at the nominating convention, said "I'm a Harriman Fan;" another example of the right message at the right time on the right product.

BUILT-IN SUBTLE

Sometimes, as with the egg-shaped L'Eggs(TM) panty hose container, the buyer can create a second use for the packaging, giving it an after life as promotional merchandise. Second only to raw macaroni and Elmer's(TM) glue, these plastic L'Eggs spheres have come to the creative rescue of virtually every gradeschooler faced with an art project due Tuesday. The containers also are at home holding bolts, earrings, and coins. Even without a logo or a message on them, the containers promote the value and the name of the panty hose that hatched from them.

SUBTLE AND INTELLIGENT

Examples of intelligent and subtle use of promotional merchandise are everywhere. Unfortunately, they are not often enough at the top of the mind of the promotional merchandise buyer, and unfortunately, becoming an intelligent and subtle buyer is something that usually is learned, not taught. Often, a very low level of "acceptable" is acceptable and the result is a 25-cent key tag with "straight-line-copy" that looks like it cost a nickel and might be used to hold someone's spare shed key.

SO SUBTLE . . .

The City of Berlin gives away small fuzzy bears about two inches high to travel agents who keep them on their desks or wear them on their lapel. A small sash that identifies the city is a giveaway that the bears represent Berlin, but the target audience of travel agents knows where the bears came from even without the sash, and the City of Berlin communicates its tourism message.

SUBTLE AND THOUGHTFUL

It is an appreciation for the combined power of the art form and the communication value that causes us to remember old Coke™ trays and tire company ashtrays as well as current promotional merchandise we see everyday. The key to producing this memorable merchandise lies, in the end, with an appreciation of the subtle influences that can be used with target audiences. After reading this far, maybe the last thing you need is another case history, but this one shows that when you take a serious look at the message promotional merchandise is conveying, startling changes can occur.

The West German ship engine manufacturer, MAN B&W Diesel, simply rethought the graphics of its cube pads. Cube pads are about as simple a product as anyone could offer and MAN B&W had used them for several years with the conventional graphics consisting of a logo near the bottom of the cube so it was still visible as the paper was used. Most buyers know enough to put the message near the bottom of a cube pad, but for most this is the end of the creative process. The same was true of the old MAN B&W graphics. However, a little thought and creativity can do a lot for a cube pad. A four-color photo of the bow of a ship is printed around the edge of the cube pad so that the ship's forward motion is part of the cube. The redesigned logo fits nicely with the total graphic, and it is still near the bottom where it will stay visible as the pad is used.

The message is clear. This is a company dedicated to ships. The target audience does not miss the message.

SUBTLE AND CLEVER

If you can't be subtle with your message be subtle in your cleverness. Midas™ mufflers—yellow scarves with the Midas logo woven into each end—are the undisputed leader in this category. Although the scarves are limited to seasonal use, they seem to have an indefinite life.

Clever use of promotional merchandise, however, is rarely as broadly accepted as the Midas™ muffler. Most of the time it is used most effectively when directed at specific target audiences who are familiar with a specific set of customs and humor. The best example of this comes from a worldwide company that asked not to have its name publicly associated with the case history.

As with all highly centralized multinational companies, people from headquarters are forever visiting the field. In this company, these headquarters managers earned the name *sea gulls* because, as one headquarters manager put it, "we would fly out to visit, eat lunch, and shit on you before we flew off again." To express their feelings, field managers had baseball caps with the word *sea gull* printed on the front. The caps were very popular with field managers and headquarters people alike because their message was clever enough to focus the irritation of field managers in an acceptable manner. The field managers obviously knew their target audience. And, with artful subtlety, they conveyed a very specific message to their audience.

SUBTLE WITH AN EYE TO ESTHETICS

Most often, subtle success comes with the help of serious attention to graphic presentation. Unfortunately, the most talented graphic artists are nowhere near the promotional merchandise industry. But as a buyer, you can bring the industry to them. Before you decide on the graphics, give the parameters—the merchandise, the message, and the audience—to an art director. This director could be working for your company's advertising agency, or you might find one through other sources. Pay the person to spend a couple hours creating a graphic design for your promotional merchandise. You could wind up with a ship on a cube pad, or better.

The entire promotional merchandise industry needs the help of a few thousand eager art directors, and corporations need to become more flexible with the use of their logos. Just because your logo must be PMS 285 red on a PMS 495 gray background on company letterhead and business cards, does not mean these are the best combinations of colors to effectively communicate a message on promotional merchandise. Here, the logo technicians have unnecessarily encumbered the message—and they have done it most likely in total ignorance of promotional merchandise. Buyers can get management to recognize the critical role art plays in promotional merchandise simply by having graphic professionals submit suggestions—whether they conform with the corporate identity book or not. The rock music video program MTV has pioneered total disregard for color and background in the use of its logo, and it has done so successfully. While you would probably not want to risk your career by suggesting MTV-esque graphics, a rational examination of the message to be communicated, the medium on which the message will live, and the audience's perception of the message, will guide you much better than a loose-leaf corporate identity book written primarily for print and signage mediums.

CONSULTANTS AND SUBTLE

There are others who may be able to help produce a promotional merchandise item that does the job you want it to do better than it would if you did it by yourself. Your public relations firm, for example, may have people who can discuss the impact of an item as well as the graphics on it.

One PR professional, Richard Wagner, is now president of Rogers Brackman, the promotional arm of Young & Rubicam advertising.

"Observing from the inside as well as the outside, the role today of promotional merchandise," he says, "is one of marketing rather than merchandising. These items are immediately cast in a broader context of something else. When you are looking in the context of a total marketing program, you can address the merchandise from this perspective."

Golin/Harris Communications, the public relations firm credited by Ray Kroc in his autobiography "Grinding It Out" with making *McDonald's* a household word, often consults with clients on the use of promotional merchandise. "We're very much at home in this capacity," says Ward White, president, Golin/Harris East.

SUBTLE BY DESIGN

Artists and designers, too, can have input into promotional merchandise. Lew Syken, owner of the Lamplight Group, a boutique New York City graphics and design studio, has earned a reputation for being able to create the environment where words and logos of corporations appear in the most effective context on merchandise. Many first-timers think Mr. Syken's job is as easy as putting down type and logos in the confines of the item's imprint area. But what Mr. Syken knows is which serifs on what type will disappear on what products, and when it is better to be big and bold instead of small. To him the only difference between your purchase of 100 clocks and your competitor's purchase of 100 clocks is what you do with the graphics on the face of your 100 clocks. He is the man who knows immediately whether the embroidery on your corduroy caps will get lost between the wales, and he knows how to beef up the letters so that the integrity of the typeface is not lost when it appears as several thousand stitches on the front of your cap.

THE ROAD TO SUBTLETY

The last consideration in promotional merchandise must be subtlety, but it is not the key, or the most important factor. Its role is universal and is applicable to disciplines far removed from geegaws and gizmos.

Subtlety in road building means there isn't a smattering of "No U Turn" signs after every intersection. Whenever you see them, it's a giveaway that a majority of drivers have missed their street, usually through bad road design, and want to turn around. The not-so-subtle point is that once you understand subtlety in promotional merchandise, you can couple its powers with your communications mandate to produce a successful promotional merchandise campaign.

INDEX